Just Another Run of the Mill Day

LEAH ATKINSON

Copyright © 2020 by Leah Atkinson

ISBN   Softcover   978-1-953537-10-2

All rights reserved. No part of this book may be reproduced or transmitted in any form or by any means, electronic or mechanical, including photocopying, recording, or by any information storage and retrieval system without express written permission from the author, except in the case of brief quotations embodied in critical reviews and certain other non-commercial uses permitted by copyright law.

Printed in the United States of America.

To order additional copies of this book, contact:
Bookwhip
1-855-339-3589
https://www.bookwhip.com

This book is dedicated as an encouragement to those who are sinking in the midst of a crisis to persevere and keep swimming!

CONTENTS

Acknowledgments vii

Prologue ix

Part 1:   The Good Ole Days 1

Part 2:   The Long and Winding Road 11

Part 3:   The Transition 77

Part 4:   The Other Shoe Drops 113

Epilogue 211

Endnotes 215

ACKNOWLEDGMENTS

I'm grateful to my wonderful husband and best friend, Steve, and my exceptional sons, Jameson and Ross, who made this book possible. Their lives have provided me with more anecdotes than I would dare ever tell, but also with poignant stories that needed to be shared. The three of them indulged my dream when I decided to attempt to write a book and then supported me throughout the entire process. I wish to thank my friends Kelli, Lois, and Priya for giving of their time to read my manuscript and offering their honest opinions and advice. I'm forever grateful to The Oley Foundation for welcoming Jameson into their wonderful organization with open arms and hearts; it truly changed his life. I'd especially like to throw out a huge thank you to Ross, who spent countless hours deciphering my handwritten thoughts and memories as he carefully typed each page, transforming the words into our family's story.

PROLOGUE

Have you ever wished, even for a moment, that your child was dead, or would simply disappear? Have those overwhelming thoughts just, from out of nowhere, invaded not only your brain but the very core of your being?

I know we as parents have all probably had those times where we would like to "kill" our children, or make them just "go away." As human beings, we naturally have feelings and certain inclinations. Who among us has not felt the heat of embarrassment when our toddler decides to lie down in the middle of our neighborhood Rite Aid store and throw a temper tantrum? Or when our precious child has to be physically carried from the church sanctuary in the middle of the service due to disruptive behavior (all the while screaming at the top of their lungs, "Please don't spank me!")?

Or how about when one of our children refuses to take "no" for an answer when demanding a toy that's very similar to one they already have at home? We've all seen this situation escalate into a total meltdown at our favorite Sam's Club or Kmart.

Then we have our adoring teenager who believes all parents must inevitably hail from Mars because we can't possibly know anything that we've been talking about or attempting to teach them.

Situations like this prompt us to utter such threats as, "When I get my hands on you, I'm going to kill you!" Or, "You are dead meat, mister!" Or, and this is my personal favorite, "I am going to wring your neck!"

Other spoken thoughts include, "Just get out of my sight!" and "I don't even want to look at you right now." But probably the most hurtful thing to say is, "The sight of you makes me sick!" And please don't try to have me believe that I'm the only parent who has ever had these emotions.

Although I'm certain I have uttered all of these aforementioned phrases at various times, plus numerous others that I haven't mentioned, that's not the type of dying or disappearing I am referring to. I'm talking *truly* dead, or gone. I mean, have you ever wished your child—your own precious flesh and blood, the person that you love more than life itself—were dead? Or lost to you forever?

Well, unfortunately, I have felt these sentiments.

I never meant to feel that way. I really consider myself to be a loving, devoted mother. And I can honestly and humbly say that I would sacrifice my life in an instant to save the life of either of my children.

As parents, it is our greatest desire that our children will always be happy and healthy, but that is not always meant to be. Some things are just out of our hands. Some circumstances seem so horrible, so incredibly hopeless and hurtful that although we don't even remotely want to entertain the thought of death or the loss of someone we love as an option, those thoughts do sometimes sneak up on us. Then we wish, for that brief moment, that it might be so.

Just be extremely careful what you wish for.

PART I

THE GOOD OLE DAYS

CHAPTER 1

You know those families depicted in Norman Rockwell's paintings—the family laughing together, celebrating special occasions together, praying together, and enjoying life together? Well, we *were* the Norman Rockwell family—a mother and a father who were authentically in love with each other, two adorable children, a dog, and a cat. We lived in a nice home in a little town in Southern Kentucky. My husband Steve and I always joked that we could have been the inspiration for one of Norman's families. Our older son even became a huge fan of Mr. Rockwell at an early age.

Franklin, Kentucky, was a typical small Southern town where newcomers were eagerly welcomed into the gentle flow of life and lasting friendships were forged with ease. Elderly gentlemen sat around the Courthouse Square and whittled the afternoons away, while children visited drugstore soda fountains for their favorite afterschool treats. We were very involved with our church, our community, our jobs, and our long-distance families, whom we had reluctantly left behind in Georgia.

Throughout the years, I had grown to love all aspects of small-town living; such was not always the case. When Steve and I first moved to Kentucky as newlyweds from our home state of Georgia, I was certain my new husband was moving me to Podunk, USA. Although as a teenager I spent much time visiting friends who lived in the country, I was still a city girl at heart. So, when visiting Franklin for the first time,

I was not impressed because we had to drive behind a very large and very slow tractor for several miles right through the middle of town. I took that as an omen, a sign of things to come. Indeed, it was an omen, but luckily, it was one of how wonderful country living could be.

Both of our sons were born while living in Kentucky. Jameson arrived in 1984, and Ross followed in 1987. And, like most young parents, we were totally devoted to our children. We loved them with an all-consuming passion. We tried not to spoil them too much; discipline was dished out when necessary. But I must say they were our whole world—two precious boys, two distinct personalities.

Jameson was a little blond-haired cutie with very pale blue eyes. Even his pediatrician would routinely comment on the unique color of his eyes. He began talking at an early age and he loved to sing. He would often sing his own versions of popular songs. Jameson also loved television shows such as *Sesame Street* and could be mesmerized for hours by watching cartoons.

Although he was a television fiend, he also enjoyed playing with action figures (especially G.I. Joes) and miniature cars. And he enjoyed the company of others while playing. Many times, Jameson would simply want me to sit and watch him while he played. We did, however, log many hours playing together with his miniature cars. He was also one of those "why" children—he asked questions about everything. He also loved to read and learn.

Ross, as a small child, was beautiful with dark brown hair and sparkling blue eyes. Everyone always commented on his little cherub face; as they say, looks can be deceiving. He may have appeared angelic on the outside, but you could be sure on the inside those little wheels were always turning. Ross had a curious sense about him; he didn't ask many questions, just got into things. He could have been the poster child for the popular Christian book *The Strong-Willed Child* written by Dr. James Dobson.

Ross was somewhat more of a challenge than his brother, though he could have a heart of gold. He was always willing to share his money or toys with others, and occasionally, he even tried to keep Jameson out of trouble. He also enjoyed using his imagination and playing, much more so than watching TV. And he definitely preferred playing alone; he rarely ever wanted me to join him during his playtime.

We lived in our wonderful little town for ten and a half years. All in all, we had a very nice life there. Then, when Jameson was eight years old and Ross was four, Steve was offered a job with a different company. The change would require us to move to Southeastern Pennsylvania. I was devastated. Moving to Pennsylvania would be like moving to a different country! I couldn't bear the thought of it. How could I pack up my children and leave our idyllic life in Kentucky? How could we take them away from the only friends they had ever known?

In June of 1992, after months of me crying and begging not to go, our family moved to Bucks County, Pennsylvania. I did manage to take a piece of our first home with us. We had been measuring the height of both boys on the inside of the nursery door since they were around fifteen months old. That door was priceless to both Steve and me. It is still with us twenty years later.

Even though Bucks County is a beautiful part of the country, I had a difficult time settling in to our new surroundings. Steve was working long hours, and I was working extremely hard to make certain that the boys adjusted to their new home—and life in general. They both seemed to do well; I was miserable. I missed my friends, I missed my family, and, let's face it, I missed the South.

Since my parents had been to visit us in September to celebrate Ross's birthday, we decided to spend Thanksgiving back in Kentucky with friends. It was a long drive, but it was wonderful seeing everyone again. The trip brightened my spirits, until it was time to leave. I honestly didn't know if I could get into our minivan and go back to Pennsylvania. I cried and cried at the very thought of it, and I'm certain I was awful to Steve.

Finally, two of my dear friends persuaded me that I had to go back, citing it was the best thing for my family. Steve swears that I cried for the entire thirteen hours it took to drive home. I believe he even offered to put me out on the side of the interstate. Of course, he didn't, although I'm certain it took great restraint on his part not to!

The following day was a turning point. After Steve had left for work (I'm sure he was anxious to get out of the house) while Jameson and Ross were at school, I had a little talk with myself. I decided then and there that I could continue to feel sorry for myself and stay miserable, or I could get over it and begin enjoying life again. I immediately phoned my friends in Kentucky to apologize for the way I had behaved, and to let them know that I was going to be just fine.

From then on, Pennsylvania was home. We had chosen our neighborhood based on the number of swing sets and basketball goals that were present; it was definitely teeming with kids. Ross and Jameson both had an abundant supply of friends to play with. Being able to enjoy the changing seasons was also a plus, especially the winter snowfalls. Living in the South didn't present much of an opportunity for snow sledding or skiing, but Pennsylvania provided all of the snow we could possibly want (although by winter's end, the thrill of shoveling snow was gone!).

Ross and Jameson were involved in almost every type of sports imaginable: baseball, soccer, roller hockey, football, karate, tennis, golf. Some sports held their interest more so than others, but most weekends we had a sporting event to attend. No matter what the weather bestowed, the game would go on.

An unexpected activity that both boys were involved in was the elementary school music program. The children were encouraged to choose and begin playing a musical instrument around the third or fourth grade. Jameson really surprised us when he came home one afternoon during his fourth grade tenure and announced he wished to play the viola. The viola? I didn't even know what that was. I was familiar with the violin, but not the viola. I learned, of course, they belong in the same instrument family.

But why would my son want to play a soft instrument? How about something a little more masculine, like a saxophone? Nope, his mind was set. He explained that it was so cool how the instructor had demonstrated it. He and his friend, Jeff, were both going to play the viola. Needless to say, his enthusiasm was short-lived. Jameson didn't grow up to play the viola or any other musical instrument.

Ross, on the other hand, was a bit more predictable. When he came from school one day, while in the third grade, and announced that he would be playing the trumpet, the world continued to rotate smoothly on its axis. We knew Ross would be destined to choose an instrument that made a lot of noise and grabbed attention. He was our wild child, and he had to play an instrument that mirrored his personality. And, unlike his brother, music would always be a mainstay in his life.

Again, for the most part, we had carved out a very nice life for ourselves. We had lived in Pennsylvania for five years when Steve was offered the opportunity to move back to our home state of Georgia. Although moving back was something that Steve and I had both hoped would someday be possible, it was a difficult decision. Moving would mean leaving friends that we cherished and a school system that was top-notch. We also hated to disrupt our sons' lives again.

Jameson and Ross were somewhat apprehensive about the move, but they assured us it would be like an adventure. Steve and I thought it would be nice to live closer to our families. So, in December of 1997, we made our move to Athens, Georgia, home of the University of Georgia Bulldawgs (and yes, I spelled it correctly). Jameson was thirteen and in the eighth grade, and Ross was ten and in the fifth grade.

The boys made friends in different stages. Jameson formed friendships at school rather quickly, but it took a while for him to really bond with anyone in our neighborhood. Once it did happen, he and his new pal were virtually inseparable for the remainder of the year. Ross, on the other hand, began meeting neighborhood kids on day one, but finding his niche at school took a little longer.

Ross also began being bullied and teased by a couple of boys in his class. I'm not sure if his small stature or just being the new kid prompted the teasing, but it made school a less than pleasant experience for him. Since he refused to tell his teacher, I discretely spoke with her and explained the situation. I don't know how she handled it, but the bullying subsided. Ross then felt comfortable at his new school.

Over the next few years, life was pretty good. As a registered nurse, I never had difficulty finding new jobs as we moved from state to state; Steve enjoyed his job as a plant manager; the boys were both in teenagedom, which definitely had its moments, but we were all surviving each new transition.

Ross, at thirteen, continued to test the waters of authority. Of course, he had always been rather stubborn and somewhat proficient at blaming others for his misdeeds. He was the type of person that if you gave him an inch, he'd take a mile; or, if you drew a line in the sand and dared him to cross it, he'd stick that grubby little toe over it every time. We loved him dearly, but he could be a handful.

Jameson was enjoying being sixteen and having a bit more freedom. He was very handsome—tall and lean, still blond, but his baby blue eyes had turned green. He had a smile that could light up the room. I guess that's why he was popular with the girls.

Unfortunately, he had begun to push the parental boundaries at times and was even questioning a few of our core values and beliefs. But all in all, he was still a pretty good kid. After all, he was a teenager, and I had heard all kinds of stories from moms of teens who had gone before me. I felt I was prepared for the battles.

Yes, all in all, we were still having a very good life. But, as the saying goes, life can change in the blink of an eye.

I blinked.

A child in crisis is a parent's worst nightmare. It doesn't matter if that child is a toddler, a teenager, or an adult. It matters not if the crisis is physical, emotional, or spiritual. It can tear their whole world apart and make yours a living hell. You feel helpless, hopeless, and totally alone, even in the midst of people you love. I know these things to be true—I've lived them. You think that things can't possibly get worse, yet they do. One child's crisis is averted, only to have you face the other child's life in shambles. As one embraces healing, the other succumbs to heartbreak. And so it goes. Life and strife are ever present, hand in hand. As parents, we deal with the ups and downs as each child presents them. Because they are our children. And a child, no matter what, is a parent's greatest blessing.

PART II

THE LONG AND WINDING ROAD

CHAPTER 2

May 1, 2001, 10:30 PM

As mentioned previously, Ross was extremely strong-willed and had a stubborn streak a mile wide. On the other hand, for every not so glamorous characteristic that he possessed, there was an equally jubilant one that shown forth. You just had to dig down beneath the surface at times to unearth them. For example, he continued to have a very giving spirit, if he was in the mood to be charitable. Also, parents and teachers alike loved him. They all thought he was a great kid. As he had gotten older, another characteristic had evolved; Ross loved to have fun. Granted, at times, he liked to have too much fun. At the tender age of thirteen, he was often considered the life of the party. I should have realized then what I was going to be in for over the next several years. If only I had known what trials lay ahead. Ignorance is, indeed, bliss.

Ross was neither organized nor very disciplined. He preferred to fly by the seat of his pants, to coin an old phrase. He was of the opinion that things would always work out, in the end. The attitude of no pain, no gain, did not have a place in Ross's life. I guess that's why it was so surprising that he had continued to practice, I use the term practice very loosely, and play the trumpet for a number of years.

During the eighth grade, Ross earned first chair trumpet in the middle school band. He also participated in jazz band.

The Malcolm Bridge Middle School Band from Watkinsville, Georgia had been invited to participate in a competition being held in Panama City Beach, Florida. The kids and the lucky chaperons, of course, would be leaving the morning of Thursday, May 3rd for their trip, and they were pumped. The thought of traveling to sunny Florida plus missing two days of school was almost too much. Only one more full day to go and paradise was within their grasp.

Ross had been anticipating the trip for weeks; no, actually months. He had been excited about it since it was first mentioned. The past few weeks it had consumed his thoughts, not to mention that in a mere three weeks after returning from the trip, school would be out for the summer. As an added bonus, in June he and Jameson were going to be student ambassadors to Europe for three weeks through the People to People Ambassador Program. Life was good! Ross had everything planned that he was going to take on the band trip—from Hawaiian shirts, to an abundance of snacks, to a toilet plunger. Yes, you heard me, a toilet plunger—a new, clean, unused one. Why a plunger? That would be used as his scepter, for we know that all kings customarily have a scepter. And, every group of middle school kids needs a king to rule them. Now it makes sense, doesn't it?

After making certain his "royal highness" had gone to bed, I went downstairs to see how the king's brother was coming along. Jameson had a research paper due the next day. Actually, he was finished with the paper itself; he just hadn't quite completed the fifty note cards that had to be turned in along with the paper. He had known about the paper for weeks, but, in true Jameson fashion, he waited until the night before the due date to complete everything. I must say though, like most typical sixteen year olds, he was somewhat amazing. Unlike me, who could barely turn on a computer, he could surf the internet, talk on the phone, instant message multiple friends simultaneously, and write note cards, all at the same time.

The day had been pretty uneventful in comparison to other days over the past few months. I had a friend who once told me that the age of fifteen was the most horrible age for teenage boys. She recounted how her son had changed, almost seemingly, right before her very eyes.

She lamented how he became defiant, argumentative, smart-mouthed, and distant. Oh, how I had dreaded that age of the damned. But alas, Jameson turned fifteen, had stayed fifteen for an entire year, and I continued to like him. Don't get me wrong, there were a few little rough patches, but for the most part, it had been a piece of cake.

Then, boom! He turned sixteen, and I would swear it seemed as though he really did change overnight. The things that I had breathed a sigh of relief about and thought that I had miraculously escaped, all came to fruition—and then some. There had been days that I was certain an alien abduction had occurred, and my new son was a droid from some distant, horrible planet.

His moods went up and down. He thought everything about his younger brother was stupid. He was constantly fighting with his girlfriend, then he was constantly trying to cheat on his girlfriend, then he dumped his girlfriend. He complained about everything. And he didn't enjoy spending time with his mom anymore. That last one really hurt. Jameson and I had always been very close, but I had become more of a bother than a mother.

One day I noticed a cut on his arm. Upon questioning him, Jameson admitted that he had intentionally cut himself with his pocket knife. When I further questioned him and asked why, he told me he had done it on several occasions; the cutting made him feel better. Around the same time, I had begun finding papers he had written detailing his desire to hurt certain people. He would also verbally talk about his desire to beat up people or cause some type of harm to them.

Steve and I were understandably upset. We both were afraid that Jameson was going to severely hurt himself or do harm to someone else. We confiscated all sharp objects from his bedroom, and we made certain that he was never home alone. Steve confided in our pastor; this resulted in an appointment being made with a Christian counselor, someone that we felt Jameson would open up to and discuss whatever was bothering him. We couldn't imagine him being so depressed or angry that he would intentionally hurt himself or anyone else, but we couldn't take any chances. Although depression was present in both of our families, Steve and I were totally blindsided by this turn of events.

Jameson wasn't thrilled with the idea of going to counseling, but he did realize he needed some type of help. We learned that Jameson wasn't suicidal, but he did obtain relief from stress through cutting. We weren't at all familiar with the ritual, and we were honestly quite shocked that Jameson had apparently been involved with this for some time. The counselor explained to us that cutting is a way some teenagers, and even some adults, try to cope with the pain of strong emotions, intense pressure, or upsetting relationship problems.

We were also told that people who cut or self-injure sometimes have other mental health problems that contribute to their emotional tension. Cutting could be associated with depression, bipolar disorder, obsessive thinking, or compulsive behaviors. Jameson's counselor felt as though there may have been some mild depression involved. He recommended that Jameson should be seen by a physician and probably placed on an antidepressant.

Jameson began seeing Dr. Tom Wells, a young doctor who, incidentally, had moved into our neighborhood. He placed Jameson on a low dose of an antidepressant and also scheduled him for frequent revisits. Jameson also continued his weekly counseling sessions. For the most part, things appeared to be improving. The mood swings were less dramatic, schoolwork was being focused on to a greater extent, and the romance had even been rekindled with the former girlfriend.

Unfortunately, there had been a few unpleasant episodes that did occur: denouncing his religious upbringing and our beliefs in general; a call from the high school guidance counselor stating that Jameson was talking about harming himself (this resulted in an emergency visit to the psychologist); and an argument with the girlfriend that resulted in a hole in my basement wall and a trip to the ER for an x-ray of his hand. We were learning to take the good with the bad.

Then came the really bad. Steve's dad had been diagnosed with lung cancer back in January; he died peacefully on the twenty-third of March. A few days before his death, Jameson's girlfriend had unexpectedly broken-up with him. The night of his granddaddy's funeral, Jameson had a meltdown—just too much was happening all at once. After that, he became somewhat of a stalker toward his ex-girlfriend—phone calls, threatening emails and letters, explosive outbursts. It became so bad that the girl's father phoned the house at 9:30 one evening stating he had to speak to us in person, right then; their church youth minister, who personally knew Jameson, accompanied him.

Turns out, Jameson had sent such an intense email to the young lady that her father was afraid Jameson was going to hurt either himself or someone else. He suggested that Jameson be admitted to the hospital for psychiatric observation; Steve and I were crushed. We honestly had no idea things had become so bad. After Steve, the father, and the youth minister had spoken at length with Jameson, he had willingly agreed to go to the hospital. Steve would accompany him while I stayed at home .We didn't want to awaken Ross and go into all the details.

After Steve and Jameson left, all I could do was cry. I had never felt so distraught in my entire life. I had lived through some very down times—deaths, unwelcomed moves, extreme loneliness—but I honestly felt as though I was being crushed and couldn't breathe. I couldn't imagine how Steve had felt; he was the one throwing his son to the lions, although it truly was for his own good.

Time crept by. Finally, after about three hours had passed, Steve called. He said Jameson had been thoroughly evaluated and was allowed to come back home. He had been deemed healthy of body, mind, and spirit. I once again sobbed, but these were sobs of relief.

Since that night, life had again been pretty much status quo. Jameson had been busy with schoolwork and spending time with Kate, his date for prom. The prom had been three nights before, on Saturday. On Sunday night, Jameson had experienced another meltdown. On Monday, after school, I had accompanied him to see Dr. Wells; his medication dosage was slightly adjusted. As I stated earlier, Tuesday had been uneventful.

At 10:30, Steve and I both were ready for bed. Out of motherly politeness, I asked Jameson if he wanted me to stay up with him, hoping beyond all hopes that he would say no (because I was very sleepy). Hallelujah! He did say no. I asked him how many more note cards he needed to write, and he answered not too many. Of course, I knew that could be anywhere between ten and forty. I kissed him on the forehead, told him I loved him, and kindly asked him not to stay up too late.

Off to bed I went.

CHAPTER 3

May 2, 2001

Jameson had awakened me at 12:50 a.m.; he told me he had a really bad stomachache. Unfortunately, these were words I'd heard many times over the past thirteen years. He'd had his first "attack" when he was just three years old, right after Ross was born.

That first night, I initially thought it had been a ploy for attention. After all, there was a new baby in the house who was receiving a lot of attention. After a short while though, it had been apparent that Jameson was indeed in a great deal of pain. I phoned a physician that I knew, and he recommended a medication to use to relieve the stomachache.

These stomachaches became an unwanted part of our family life. There was no "rhyme or reason" to when they occurred, although it seemed most of them happened late at night or during the middle of the night. They would cause Jameson to loudly moan and groan, writhe around on the floor, and cry in pain. And these episodes would sometimes last for hours. As he got older, the pain had actually seemed to intensify. No matter what medication the pediatrician prescribed, nothing seemed to alleviate or even ease the pain.

Finally, when Jameson was in the first grade, I talked the pediatrician into performing an upper gastrointestinal (GI) x-ray and a barium enema. I realized that these tests wouldn't be very pleasant for a six-year-old to have to undertake, but by that time I had been desperate to find a cause for his agony. Jameson was a trooper. He tolerated the tests well. They both came back negative.

The pediatrician commented that the only thing abnormal that had shown up on the x-rays was the location of Jameson's appendix. Normally, a person's appendix is located in the lower right quadrant of your abdomen, attached to your large intestine. Jameson's was located up high in his right side, close to his ribcage. The doctor also stated that this fact wouldn't be the cause of Jameson's stomachaches. He suggested we try biofeedback as a solution to Jameson's problem. I changed pediatricians.

The stomachaches continued rather frequently for the next two years. They actually seemed to worsen after Steve accepted a job with a new company and had to move to Pennsylvania a few months ahead of us. Surely the original pediatrician hadn't been on the right track. No, he had not! I had witnessed all of Jameson's episodes, and I positively knew they weren't in his head.

But, I definitely felt like a guilty, uncaring mother. The longer these episodes continued, the more frustrated I had become. And the more frustrated I had become, the less caring I was. While Jameson would be battling with the pain and discomfort, I would be wishing his pain would ease off so *I* could get some sleep. He had gotten to the point when, at times, he would cry out that he was going to die. I would flippantly reassure him that he wasn't going to die, all the while thinking, "But I might kill him if he doesn't calm down." If only we could undo the wrongs we have done, especially to the people we love the most.

A few weeks before we had made our official move to Pennsylvania, I had an appointment with our family physician and was lamenting about Jameson's situation. The doctor commented that his symptoms sounded like an ulcer and recommended a pediatric gastroenterologist located in Nashville. It felt somewhat senseless to see this doctor only once since we were preparing for our move. But at this point, I had been willing to try anything.

The specialist was nice and appeared very thorough. He too, believed that Jameson was suffering from a stomach ulcer. Since he wouldn't be able to treat Jameson long-term, his recommendation was for Jameson to take the medication Zantac regularly for six months. The effectiveness or ineffectiveness of the Zantac would determine if an ulcer was, indeed, the problem.

Miraculously, after beginning the Zantac, the stomachaches subsided and appeared resolved. Coincidentally, if Jameson didn't take his Zantac regularly, he would have occasional problems. Some of these attacks were worse than others. But over time, the incidence of these grew less and less. It had actually been close to a year since Jameson had been troubled with a bad stomachache. Oh well, I guess our luck couldn't hold out forever.

By the time I had awakened myself enough to join him, Jameson was doubled over in the middle of the bathroom floor. He decided to lie in the bathtub and soak in hot water for a while in order to try and ease the discomfort (this was a trick his daddy had taught him). After only a few minutes in the tub, he felt as though he needed to throw up. "Good," I thought. Vomiting usually helped to ease him off. He vomited an extremely large amount. No relief.

He continued to be doubled over with pain. He also stated that this was the worst one that he could ever remember having. Even though the pain really wasn't localized, I had a fleeting thought of appendicitis. I checked his temperature—97.5 degrees (subnormal, of course). He moved from the bathroom to the bed, back to the bathroom, and then back to the bed. Several bouts of the dry heaves had occurred. He had also thought a couple of times that the pain was beginning to ease off, only to have it come back with a vengeance.

I had really begun to have a feeling that this was something more than just one of his routine attacks. At 2:30 a.m., we decided we needed to make a trip to the emergency room. At Jameson's request, I ran any red light we came upon. I already had to convince him to put on clothes for the trip; he felt so bad he didn't care if he was naked or not. We arrived at the ER at 3:00 a.m.

While I checked him in, it was impossible for Jameson to get comfortable in any position in the waiting room chairs. I believe he tried every possible position. He resorted to lying on the floor. The security guard then paid a little visit and told Jameson that being on the floor was a no-no.

It was going to be a long night.

CHAPTER 4

May 2, 2001

After what I'm sure seemed like an eternity to Jameson, we were taken back to an ER exam room. The stretcher bed was none too comfortable, but it was better than the waiting room chairs. An ER doctor came in shortly thereafter, introduced himself, and examined Jameson. I tried to give him some background history, maybe something to help him determine how to relieve my son's anguish.

After the doctor had completed his initial evaluation of Jameson, a male nurse came in and started an IV (intravenous fluid therapy). Of course, he started it in the crook of Jameson's arm. As for the patient's comfort, that was the worst possible place for an IV because you have to keep your arm perfectly straight, or the IV won't infuse. Oh well, the IV needle would only be in place for a short time. For pain and nausea control, Jameson was given a combination of three medications: Phenergan, Toradol, and Zofran.

It took almost an hour for the medications to take any effect. In the meantime, Jameson acquired a roommate. We didn't actually see the patient because each area in the large exam room was quarantined off using curtains. By the sound of her voice, this new roomie appeared to be a middle- aged woman. And we heard the sound of her voice a lot! For the next couple of hours, she moaned and cried and called for the nurse and moaned and cried some more. Now, I don't want to sound uncaring or unkind, but we were having our own little crisis situation across the room. And her situation didn't do a lot to help ours.

While waiting for his medications to work miracles, Jameson wriggled and squirmed and worried about what time it was. He apologized to me several times for having to go to the trouble to take him to the ER, and he worried if I would feel like going to work the next day. I tried to assure him that neither was any problem. He was also worried about getting his research paper turned in and about missing his morning classes. I told him not to worry about his classes; he could get some sleep and go in to school in time for English class and turn in his paper. During all of his pain and discomfort, he had also thought enough about me to ask the nurse to bring me a blanket; I was freezing because the ER felt like a meat locker in the middle of Antarctica. In relation to the sub-zero indoor climate, I was regularly pulling the covers back on Jameson because he was constantly moving around and knocking them off. Each time that I would re-cover him, he would thank me. Although the circumstances were less than stellar, it was comforting to realize my son still had concern for others and not just himself.

Once the "female noise machine" from across the room had been transferred elsewhere, Jameson had finally drifted off to sleep. After he had slept for about thirty minutes, an attendant came and took him to have an x-ray done on his abdomen. After returning from the x-ray department, he continued dozing. Within the next few minutes the ER doctor returned. He informed me that Jameson's potassium level was low and that his white blood cell count was elevated to 26,000. Since a normal white cell count is usually in the range of 5,000 to 7,000, I knew that meant that Jameson had a raging infection somewhere in his body.

The doctor also said something about the x-ray showing pockets of liquid in Jameson's abdominal cavity, which he explained wasn't normal. He continued by saying he'd like to admit Jameson to the hospital and run some more tests because he felt something wasn't right. A feeling of uneasiness had begun to settle over me. I had thought I would bring Jameson to the ER, he would be given something for pain, we'd hang around for a while, and then we'd go back home. And then the doctor began talking admission to the hospital. He told me he would consult with the doctor on call and then get back to me.

Jameson continued to doze. After twenty more minutes had passed, the ER doctor, after consulting the on-call doctor, said it had been decided that definitely the best thing was to admit Jameson and run some tests. Also, a gastroenterologist was going to be called in on the case. After the doctor left, since Jameson appeared to be resting comfortably at the moment, I stepped outside of the hospital and called Steve on my cell phone to tell him what was going on. Shortly after I returned to the ER, at around 6:10 a.m., Jameson was admitted to the 4th floor, room 408.

It had been a very long night indeed.

CHAPTER 5

May 2, 2001

After spending a large portion of the night in the ER, Jameson was happy to be in a private room and lying in a real hospital bed instead of the narrow, hard ER stretcher that he had been attempting to sleep on.

To our good fortune, Dr. Wells, Jameson's primary care physician, was the doctor on call for Wednesday. He was in to see Jameson bright and early at about 6:30 a.m. He had already spoken with the ER doctor and reviewed Jameson's x-rays and lab results. He said he was going to order an abdominal computed tomography (CT) scan for later in the morning. He then explained that he wasn't certain if he would be calling in a GI specialist or a general surgeon to see Jameson because at that point it was unclear what the problem was.

In order for a CT scan to be done, Jameson had to drink a large quantity of contrast medium—a barium sulfate suspension—in order for the images to come out clearly, but that was a problem: (*a*) the contrast didn't taste good; (*b*) as I said before, a large quantity of contrast had to be drunk; and (*c*) all Jameson wanted to do was sleep. He wasn't the least bit interested in drinking large amounts of anything, much less something that tasted bad.

The next few hours were spent with Jameson sleeping off and on, him being encouraged to drink more contrast each time he woke up, and me nervously flipping the TV channels. I had spoken with Steve a second time to tell him what little I knew. He was scheduled to work overnight that night due to some special training sessions. Since Steve would be gone overnight and I wasn't quite sure what was going on with Jameson, I had also phoned my parents (who lived out of town) to tell them about Jameson and ask if they could come to Athens and spend the night with Ross. At that point, I didn't suspect anything serious happening with Jameson, but I did anticipate him being in the hospital until the next morning.

At around 11:00 a.m., Jameson's primary nurse came into the room and informed us that if he didn't finish drinking the contrast, she would have to insert a nasogastric (NG) tube into his nose and pour the rest of the contrast through it. Until now, I had been hesitant to awaken him too often because I knew when he was sleeping that he was also comfortable. But now, I also knew this nurse was serious about the NG tube. I awakened him and cheered him on to finish drinking the contrast. It took a lot of cheering on! I had also given him a few sips of water because he was so thirsty and kept begging me for water. As a nurse, I knew I shouldn't have given him the water, and I also knew his primary nurse would have shot me if she had known; as a mom, I didn't care.

About this same time, I had also begun to notice that Jameson was looking somewhat pale and that his stomach had become a little distended. I called Steve back and asked him to come to the hospital; something just didn't feel right. Also, Jameson wanted him to bring his research paper so he could finish a few things on it. He then wanted Steve to take it to school and turn it in for him. Getting that research paper turned in on time was a big concern for him. While I tried to reassure him that he would certainly, under the circumstances, be allowed to turn the paper in late, he was adamant that it had to be on time. He explained to me that he himself had jokingly asked if being in the hospital would be a good enough excuse for the paper to be turned in late, to which his teacher had replied that no, even that would not be good enough. It looked like Steve would be making a trip to the school.

Between 11:30 a.m. and noon, I went to the nurses' station to let them know that Jameson had finally finished drinking the contrast and, also, to ask when he would be taken down to x-ray. I was told that someone from the x-ray department would be coming to get him in a few minutes. In the meantime, Steve had arrived at the hospital (with the research paper); and Jameson had added a few more details to his paper. He then basically ordered Steve to deliver his paper to the school.

Meanwhile, I continued to wait for Jameson to be taken to x-ray to have his CT scan done. By this time, Jameson was having no pain; but he was feeling uncomfortable. Around 2:00 p.m., just a few minutes after Steve returned to the hospital, Jameson was taken down for his scan. Steve and I, of course, followed him downstairs to the x-ray department. I had begun to feel even more ill at ease about the entire situation.

When the x-ray technician took Jameson in to have his scan done, we were told it would take approximately fifteen to twenty minutes for it to be completed. While we were waiting, we asked if our neighbor who was a radiologist at the hospital, Dr. Kevin Spangler, was working. We were told that he was at work, but that he wasn't working in the CT area. The x-ray tech then told us she would call Dr. Spangler and let him know we were there and were asking for him.

Kevin arrived in the CT area in just a few minutes. He sat and talked to us and we filled him in on what was happening. He stayed with us for a while, then he went into the area where Jameson was having his scan done. The scan was taking much longer than the anticipated fifteen to twenty minutes, and Steve and I were both getting antsy.

After Kevin studied the scan results, he came back out into the hallway and explained to us that Jameson had an intestinal blockage and that he was going to need surgery as soon as it could be arranged. He said he was going to call Dr. Wells right away in order to get things moving. When Jameson was wheeled back out into the hallway, he was sitting in the wheelchair, not looking too spectacular. I remember Kevin going over to him and asking him how he felt, and Jameson replying, "not too good." Kevin then told Jameson that they were going to take care of him.

We followed Jameson back up to room 408. Now, as a nurse, I was familiar with intestinal blockages, in older people that is. I had never had a younger patient with an intestinal blockage and certainly not a teenager. I did know that the section of the intestine containing the blockage would have to be surgically removed; I assumed maybe a foot, two feet at the most, would be affected.

When Jameson got back into bed, he said he felt like he was going to vomit. He was fussing at me to hurry up and get him something to throw up in. I grabbed the trashcan out of the bathroom, but I was too late. Puke went all over the floor, and on my right shoe.

Jameson calmly said, "I told you to hurry up."

CHAPTER 6

May 2, 2001

Immediately after Jameson's vomiting episode, a nurse's aide came into the room. I apologized about the condition of the floor and explained it apparently was my fault. After she graciously cleaned up our mess, she took Jameson's vital signs (temperature, pulse, blood pressure). His blood pressure registered 54/40 on the electronic blood pressure cuff machine.

When the aide told me what his blood pressure was, I told her there was no way that the reading could be correct (I knew blood pressure that low was extremely dangerous) . I asked the aide to please go and get a different blood pressure machine and retake it. After she left the room, I continued to insist to Steve that it was impossible for the reading to be correct.

A very few moments later, the charge nurse, along with Jameson's primary nurse, came rushing into his room. The charge nurse hurriedly explained that they were taking Jameson to the intensive care unit (ICU). At approximately the same time, Dr. Wells came into the room. He tried to briefly explain Jameson's situation to us. Apparently, Jameson's condition was so very serious that he was beginning to go into shock; his blood pressure was indeed only 54/40.

Dr. Wells continued to explain that Jameson required emergency surgery and asked if we had a surgeon preference.

Steve and I had no idea who to use, so Dr. Wells recommended Dr. Cody Gunn. He explained that Dr. Gunn was the surgeon that he would trust to operate on his own children. Without hesitation, we went along with his recommendation.

Jameson was rushed off to the ICU, with Steve and me right with him. We didn't even stop to see if we were allowed into the unit, we just went in. We were asked to stand out of the way. Even with all of my years of nursing experience, I still didn't fully grasp how serious the situation was. It was as if my logical thinking had just shut down; it seemed that my mind and body were separate entities.

Jameson was pretty much out of it by this point. He was hooked up to a variety of monitors. Several different IV lines were started on him simultaneously with various types of fluids and medications being pumped into his body. His blood pressure remained drastically low, and his heart rate was very rapid. His body was in full-blown shock. There were about eight doctors and nurses working on him.

After several minutes his vital signs began to stabilize somewhat, and we were allowed to go over and see him. Jameson was a little more alert but was talking somewhat incoherently. All of the sudden he exclaimed, "I just felt my heart stop!" I tried to reassure him that he was okay; I didn't realize how close he was to the truth.

When Jameson had stabilized enough, the attending staff moved him from his bed to a stretcher in order to take him to the operating room. As they were moving him, he evidently had the feeling that he was falling. He was emphatically saying, "Whoa, whoa!" The nurses assured him that they were just moving him onto a stretcher and that he wasn't going to fall. Even at Death's door, the boy could bring a smile to my face.

After moving onto the stretcher, he was hurriedly rushed off to the operating room (OR). Dr. Wells was in such a rush to get him there that he himself willingly helped push the stretcher.

Everything happened so quickly, I honestly don't remember if we even got the chance to reassure Jameson, to hold his hand, to tell him how much we loved him.

I learned that when you are in a daze, your memory doesn't function well.

CHAPTER 7

May 2, 2001

After Jameson was wheeled into the OR, Steve and I were shown to the surgery waiting room. We were told that we would be called when the surgery began and that we would receive updates throughout the surgery. I knew Jameson was going to require an intestinal resection based on the brief information that Kevin Spangler had given us earlier. I went over the procedure with Steve, explaining that Dr. Gunn would cut out the portion of the intestine that was affected, and then he would reattach the two ends back together. I estimated that probably one or two feet of intestine would have to be removed and also stated that this was a pretty common type of surgery (although not very common in sixteen-year-olds).

Dr. Spangler came and joined us for a while in the waiting room. He tried to explain to us what had happened with Jameson and the cause. He said, apparently Jameson had a condition called intestinal malrotation, which was a congenital abnormality. He went on to explain that in utero, the intestines are formed outside of the body at the base of the umbilical cord. As the intestine returns to the abdominal cavity, it makes two rotations and becomes fixed into its normal position, with the small intestine centrally located in the abdomen and the large intestine draping around the top and sides of the small intestine.

As in Jameson's case, malrotation occurs when the rotation process is incomplete and the large intestine doesn't attach to the right lower abdominal wall as it normally does. In patients with malrotation the large intestine is located to the right of the abdomen, while the small intestine is on the left of the abdomen. Since the intestine is not properly fixated, it may twist and cut off its own blood supply. This is called a volvulus, and this is what happened to Jameson. At that moment, it was crystal clear why Jameson had been plagued with severe stomachaches throughout his life. His problems hadn't been caused by an alleged ulcer; his intestines had been twisting upon themselves all along. No wonder the pain had been so intense. This also explained the strange location of his appendix.

After Kevin had stayed with us for a while, we encouraged him to go home, and we thanked him profusely for being there for us and especially for Jameson. News about Jameson had apparently spread rather quickly. After Kevin left, several people made their way to the hospital. Reverend Crist Camden, our church pastor, was the first to arrive. He had already been by to check on Jameson earlier in the day, before the situation became a bit more serious.

A couple of Jameson's female friends, after hearing the news earlier in the day while at school, stopped by. My parents arrived from out of town, ready to stay with Ross for the night, but totally unaware that Jameson was in the midst of surgery. Everything had happened so suddenly, I hadn't gotten the chance to phone them before they left their house. Other people showed up during the surgery, including Ross, Jameson's girlfriend, Kate, one of his best friends, Greg, and one of my best friends, Karen.

Our initial call from the OR didn't take place until sometime after the surgery had gotten underway. We were told that Jameson was doing fine, and that we would receive another call later. As we sat there waiting, I began to worry that Jameson might not be recovered enough from his surgery to go on his European trip.

Oh, if only we had known the true trauma that was taking place in that OR! Surgery apparently had begun around 5:10 p.m. and ended about 7:20 p.m. I remember commenting that was a relatively short time for a major surgery.

Almost immediately after we had received the call from the OR, letting us know that the surgery was over, Dr. Gunn came into the waiting room. When he strongly recommended that he talk with Steve and me in private instead of in front of our family and friends, I knew something was wrong.

Dr. Gunn led us into a small, private room and closed the door. The next few moments were the most horrible of my entire life. We were listening intently to what he was saying to us, but it was so surreal. It was as though he couldn't possibly be telling us the devastating news that was spilling out of his mouth.

He said the situation had been much worse than he ever could have expected; he had to concentrate on just saving Jameson's life, most of the small intestine had been necrotic due to its blood supply being cut off, had to remove all but approximately three feet, still didn't know if Jameson would pull through, the next 24- 48 hours would be critical, a permanent IV would be required for nutrition, Jameson may never be able to eat again, different types of IV devices could be used, the main goal during surgery was to save Jameson's life. We both sat there numb. I felt as though my brain wasn't functioning; I honestly couldn't comprehend all that he had told us.

How could this possibly be happening? Jameson had been healthy as a horse, and now we might lose him?! Steve and I just held each other and cried. What else could you do when you'd just been told that your precious son might not live, and even if he did his life would be completely, horribly changed forever.

It's funny what goes through your mind at odd times. I really don't know exactly what should've been going through my mind at that exact moment, but I was thinking, "Oh, God! He may not be able to swim on the swim team anymore. That would kill him!" The swim team had been such an important part of his life.

I was in despair. After just hearing everything Dr. Gunn had told us, I had my fleeting thought, "Jameson would be better off dead than to have to live such a miserable existence!" I knew as soon as I thought it, that was *not* how I felt, but I couldn't prevent myself from thinking it, however briefly it was.

In that next moment I was determined, no matter what, that Jameson would be back on the swim team his senior year. And he would eat his favorite foods. And he would enjoy all the things that other sixteen-year-olds enjoyed. And even though I honestly felt like I could die, I somehow knew that Jameson wouldn't.

I would just have to trust God to bring him through.

CHAPTER 8

May 2, 2001

After Dr. Gunn left us, Steve and I remained in the solitude of the private little room for a few moments longer. We both had a difficult time grasping the magnitude of the information that had just been given to us. After we had somewhat composed ourselves, we had the daunting task of telling everyone, especially Ross and my parents, just how critical the situation was.

When we walked back into the surgery waiting room, I broke down again. Through my sobs, the only words I could speak were, "It's bad. It's really bad!" I was then able to regain control of myself, and we somehow relayed the news of Jameson's crisis. By this time, Wednesday night prayer services at our church had ended, so the waiting room was almost filled with friends from church who had heard the news and wanted to come to the hospital and lend their support.

Steve also had the difficult job of calling his family, particularly his mom, and telling them about Jameson. Steve's oldest brother had been killed in 1978, and his dad had just lost his battle with cancer on March 23. Now there was a possibility that his mom might also lose her grandson. The news was especially hard on her.

After all of the phone calls were made and prayers had been offered up on Jameson's behalf, we all remained together for the next hour while he was in the recovery room. We spent this hour crying, consoling each other and being consoled. It was an absolute nightmare.

When Jameson was finally brought out of recovery and taken to the ICU, Dr. Gunn met Steve and me at the intensive care unit. He explained that normally patients in the ICU weren't allowed to have any visitors stay overnight with them. He then went on to say that Jameson's situation was so touch and go, he wanted both of us to stay throughout the night. He explained that there was a chance Jameson wouldn't survive until the morning, and he knew we would want to stay with him.

When we were finally allowed to see Jameson, he had tubes and IVs everywhere and was hooked up to all sorts of monitors, but he looked good. He looked really good. His color was good, and he appeared comfortable. He was on a ventilator, which Dr. Gunn had explained he would stay on until at least Friday in order that his body would have to do as little work as possible. Steve counted fifteen tubes of various types either exiting Jameson's body or entering it.

After a while, Ross and my parents were also allowed into the unit to see him for a brief time. The news had been devastating to my parents. They both were very close to Jameson, but especially my dad. He had been like Jameson's best friend growing up. The three of them spent the night in a little waiting room near the ICU because Ross wanted to be close by during the night. This indeed demonstrated some level of devotion to Jameson on Ross's behalf; he had always hated even stepping inside a hospital.

Dr. Gunn had also explained that Jameson would be kept very sedated, literally knocked out, in order to allow his body as much rest as possible. He stated that rest was imperative due to the amount of trauma his body had withstood. We were also told that Jameson would be going back into surgery on Friday morning in order to see how things were looking on the inside. Dr. Gunn also reiterated that the next twenty-four to forty-eight hours were critical.

God, please help us all.

CHAPTER 9

May 3, 2001

Jameson actually had a very good first night in the ICU. Nurses were in and out rather frequently, changing his position, giving him pain medicine, adjusting IVs, monitoring his vital signs. Steve and I kept vigil throughout the night; he in a reclining chair and me on a loveseat. We each would occasionally doze off for short periods of time; but with every movement or noise that Jameson made, we both were wide-awake in an instant. Looking back, it's apparent that we both were in a dazed mental state that first night. After the three of us were settled into "our" room in the intensive care unit, Steve and I were chuckling about how we bet God had now gotten Jameson's attention for doubting His existence. Can you believe it? We were actually talking about God getting even and, worse still, we were laughing about it! I think the old adage about laughing to keep from crying was really the motivating factor behind our conversation. We knew God didn't cause this catastrophe to befall Jameson, but the fact was we were scared to death that we were going to lose him. Since we couldn't bring ourselves to discuss that possibility, our discussion centered on God's punishment (according to our altered mental statuses).

Jameson woke up a few times, and the ventilation tube down his throat would cause him to panic—it made him feel as if he was choking and couldn't breathe. To make the situation even more frightening, both of his hands were tied down to the bed using restraints in order to prevent him from inadvertently pulling out any of the tubes or IVs. Due to the emergency nature of his surgery, he also had no idea what had happened to him and what was taking place in the aftermath. Although he was very groggy, we tried to briefly explain to him his situation. He could only stay awake for a few minutes at a time, and though he didn't appear to be in much pain, the fear in his eyes was heart-wrenching. He was given plenty of kisses, caresses, and reassurances throughout the night. And I remained in a state of disbelief that my Jameson would actually have to fight for his life.

Come morning, the horror of the previous night still hung heavy over us. But, thank God, Jameson had conquered the first few hours and his condition had stabilized. He continued to be awake for only short intervals due to the heavy doses of medication, but his fear and panic seemed to have subsided.

The day was filled with an incomprehensible number of visitors, quite a few who were actually allowed into the unit to visit Jameson. There were only a few people allowed in to visit at any one time, but during visiting hours there was always a steady stream in and out to see him. Some of the visitors were friends from school that I had never even seen before. Steve's mom and his siblings had arrived early in the morning. The nursing staff was very accommodating and patient. I don't think they were accustomed to having a teenager as a houseguest.

There was an entire waiting room full of people throughout the day. Friends brought in food for our family (and for whomever else needed to eat). My parents graciously took upon themselves the duty of overseeing Ross's needs. His middle school band was scheduled to leave early afternoon and travel to the band competition in Panama City for the weekend (this was one of the most popular beaches in the South). Steve and I had decided to allow Ross to go on the trip as planned, with frequent updates about Jameson being passed along to my friend who was chaperoning the trip. My mama made certain everything was packed for the trip, and my daddy drove Ross to the school to meet his bandmates. I'm sure it did my parents good to have a distraction for a while; they were extremely upset about Jameson.

The number of visitors during the day didn't compare with the large number present that evening. A lot of the same people from church who had been with us the night before were back again. And I think it's safe to say that the entire youth group was present and accounted for. The hospital staff herded people into a nearby conference room, just so the hallway wouldn't be obstructed. If there is one thing that Jameson should have learned from this experience, it was that he was very much loved and cared for (we also had ex-girlfriends all over the place!).

Since Jameson couldn't speak due to being intubated, he quickly became proficient with hand gestures and spelling out words with his finger (he was allowed to have his hand unrestrained during the day while everyone was alert). One such demonstration of his communication abilities occurred after I had been out of the room for no more than 10-15 minutes. I had been desperate for a shower, since not having had one for more than forty-eight hours. The nurses graciously allowed me to use a walk-in shower located down the hall from the intensive care unit. In retrospect, they were probably so gracious because they hoped it would help my looks.

Anyway, when I walked back into Jameson's room after my wonderful shower, I was met with a scowl. Even though Jameson had several visitors keeping him company while I was out of the room, I could tell he was not a happy camper. My mama had told him I was just down the hall taking a shower and that I would be right back, but that didn't seem to sit too well with him. He jabbed his index finger in my direction, and then pointed at his bed. When I asked him what he meant, he again forcefully thrust his index finger toward me, and then just as forcefully toward his bed.

"I don't think he liked you leaving his room," explained my mama.

"You want me to stay in your room?" I questioned.

With tears in his eyes, he emphatically nodded his head. It was then that I realized how truly scared and upset he must have been. And he had every right to be. His entire life changed in a matter of hours, and nothing would ever be the same again. Not ever. Steve and

I tried to explain to him what had happened, but we were both still pretty confused ourselves. How could Jameson have been expected to comprehend the magnitude of the previous day's events? There was no conceivable way he could've had a handle on the situation. He knew he was confined to a hospital bed, experiencing a sadistic combination of pain, weakness, and mind -numbing medications, and was in the grip of numerous tubes and mechanical devices.

He had been given many words of comfort and encouragement in an attempt to calm his fears and boost his spirits. I wonder, did he think he was going to die? Did he think that all of the well-meaning words were just an attempt to ease his passing? Did he think he may never see these friends and family members again? Did he think that God had betrayed him, and that maybe, as a form of punishment for some past transgression, he was going to be allowed to die?

We don't know exactly what he was thinking, because he couldn't verbally communicate with us. Along with spelling out words with his finger, we also reverted to our special quiet symbol of many years before, used when Jameson was a little boy. When we would be in church, or any other place where talking was inappropriate, and we wanted to convey "I love you" to each other, we would squeeze the other's hand three times. That precious gesture was indeed a lifeline that first post-op day.

Earlier in the day, when Dr. Gunn had made rounds, we learned that he had consulted with a GI specialist that he knew from med school, a Dr. Robert Martindale. This surgeon was apparently at the top of the field when it came to any type of gastrointestinal problem. He was the head of the GI department at the Medical College of Georgia located in Augusta, Georgia, and also traveled the world doing lectures and presentations at various medical conferences. Dr. Gunn had consulted him due to the extreme nature of the surgery and the delicate condition that Jameson was in.

At Dr. Martindale's recommendation, Dr. Gunn had decided during Friday's surgery not to reattach the two ends of the small intestine back together as he had originally planned but instead to create a temporary ostomy in order to allow the intestine to heal maximally. For those who are unsure, an ostomy is formed when part of the intestine is surgically brought through the abdominal wall to the outside of the abdomen and the body's waste is collected into a bag (in other words, poop freely drains into the ostomy bag and the bag is emptied as needed). Even Jameson's new diagnosis had a particularly crude name—short bowel syndrome or dumping syndrome.

The idea of an ostomy struck fear in me. Three of my closet relatives, including my mother, had lived with ostomies. I really didn't know how Jameson would react to something so gross and disgusting. Of course, I would come to find that Jameson would react to this the same way he would react to most everything else—with bravery, extreme courage, non-complaining, finding humor in any situation, and in the end, victory.

Okay, if that was what would be best for Jameson, then so be it.

CHAPTER 10

May 4, 2001

Thirty-six hours had passed since his initial surgery, and Jameson seemed to be doing well. There we were at his bedside, preparing for him to undergo a second surgery. Could this poor child actually be strong enough to withstand the trauma of a second surgery, so soon after the life-threatening first one? Were Steve and I emotionally strong enough to make it through this second surgery?

There were several of us at his bedside: Steve, myself, Mama, Daddy, and Brother Crist. Jameson surprised me by finger spelling and asking if Ross would be there. He nodded his head in understanding when I explained to him why his brother couldn't be. As we laid our hands on my precious child, held his hand, and listened as Brother Crist prayed over him, the words to the beautiful old hymn "It is Well With my Soul" just kept playing over in my mind, and I felt at peace. I knew everything was well, and that everything would turn out all right.

> When peace like a river, attendeth my way.
> When sorrows like sea billows roll;
> Whatever my lot, Thou hast taught me to say,
> "It is well, it is well, with my soul."
> It is well, with my soul,

It is well, with my soul,
It is well, it is well, with my soul.

After the prayer was finished, Jameson broke my heart. He spelled out with his finger, "I'm scared." We hugged him and kissed him some more, and I told him since I couldn't be in the operating room with him during surgery, God was going to be there with him, with His arms wrapped tightly around him, hugging him close, and taking care of him the whole time.

Then, Jameson helped pull me back together. Again, writing with his finger, he spelled out, "I'm ready." I believe my child began maturing into a man at that very moment.

Just a few minutes later, several nurses and attendants came into the room to take Jameson to the operating room. One of the nurses explained that once the ventilator was turned off, Jameson wouldn't be able to breathe on his own because of the intubation tube down his throat. On the trip to the OR, a nurse would use an Ambu bag connected to the intubation tube to manually provide oxygen to Jameson until he could be reconnected to a ventilator once in the OR. Steve and I were also told we could accompany Jameson as far as the entrance to the operating room.

Jameson was readied to go; IV pumps were unplugged, the bed was adjusted and unplugged, monitors were disconnected, and lastly the ventilator machine was disconnected. The nurse quickly positioned the Ambu bag and began manually pumping it in order to allow Jameson to breathe. The other attendants began rolling the bed, foot first, through the doorway of the room, with Steve and I following.

There was one slight problem—the doorway wasn't wide enough for a person and the bed to fit through at the same time. The nurse squeezing the Ambu bag had no choice but to remove the life-sustaining device from the intubation tube and stand aside while the bed was moved through the doorway. I could only imagine what was going through Jameson's mind; I was in a near-panic. The entire scenario lasted only a few seconds, but to me it seemed like an eternity. I was acutely aware that Jameson couldn't breathe, and my eyes were focused on his face; his expression never changed. Then the nurse was back at his side and administering the precious oxygen once again.

When we arrived at the OR doors, both Steve and I kissed Jameson on his forehead, told him we loved him, and watched him disappear into the OR. He had seemed very calm on the elevator ride; that had helped Steve and me remain calm. We then headed to the surgery waiting room.

There were approximately twenty-five to thirty friends and family at the hospital that morning for Jameson's surgery. We all visited among each other, making small talk, relaying humorous stories, and half-heartedly watching the morning news on the TV. We were very anxious over the impending outcome of this surgery, although I have to say I continued to have a feeling of peace over me.

The surgery lasted around two hours. When it was over, Dr. Gunn came to the waiting room and called Steve and me into the hallway, and not into a little private room. He immediately said, "It couldn't have gone any better."

Hallelujah! Quite a different report from the one we had received a mere thirty-six hours ago. Dr. Gunn continued by saying that there were a few places in Jameson's small intestine that still looked questionable, but he did say that he was optimistic. He explained that the next ten days would be the determining factor. If no fever or ill-effects presented themselves during that time frame, he thought we would be in the clear.

After Dr. Gunn left, Steve and I told our family and friends the good news. Everyone was ecstatic! Prayers were being answered. People confidently went to work and back to school. All of a sudden, I felt starved. While Jameson was in the recovery room, a small group of us went to the hospital cafeteria and ate the first decent meal we'd had in days. Shortly thereafter, Jameson returned to the ICU from the recovery room. He continued to have a large number of tubes and IVs, but he was taken off of the ventilator, and spontaneously began breathing on his own.

That was a very proud moment indeed!

CHAPTER 11

May 4, 2001

Jameson was very alert after returning from the recovery room. He was having some pain, but his biggest complaint was a sore throat which had been caused by the endotracheal tube down his throat. Of course, he was so happy to be rid of it and to be able to talk again; he didn't complain much about anything. He later told me that having that tube down his throat was the worst thing he had ever experienced. He described it as a constant feeling of choking and of feeling like he was suffocating. Not an experience that a mother would want her son to have to go through. Shortly after Jameson's return to his room in the ICU, the barrage of visitors began again. Even though they were coming in only two or three at a time, I knew he didn't need to be having so much company. At the same time, my heart told me that the visitors were good for him—they were keeping his mind off himself and also showing him just how much he was cared about.

On the day following his first surgery, Dr. Gunn explained to Steve and me that if we would prefer to have Jameson transferred to a bigger hospital in Atlanta, he would understand and would set the transfer in motion. We thanked him for offering but assured him that we believed Jameson was receiving the best possible care available right where he was. We had been told by various people that Dr. Gunn was the best surgeon in Athens, and we had begun to see that for ourselves. Besides, we knew if Jameson was transferred to Atlanta, it would cause his number of visitors to greatly decline. We believed having his friends around would contribute almost as much to his healing as the medical care he received.

Just as Dr. Gunn had told us on the previous day, Jameson came back from surgery with a newly formed jejunostomy, or just ostomy for short. As explained earlier, this procedure was done in order to give Jameson's intestinal tract the proper rest and time to heal. Jameson's ostomy was formed using the second portion of the small intestine, known as the jejunum (hence the name jejunostomy). The plan was for the ostomy to be in place for approximately three months, at which time the two ends of the small intestine would be surgically reattached.

We had explained to Jameson what was going to be done and what to expect, but I really didn't know how he was going to react when he actually saw the ostomy. They are not one of the more appeasing parts of the body for the human eye to behold. I didn't have to worry about his reaction for very long.

Early in the afternoon, the hospital's wound and ostomy nurse came to pay Jameson a visit. She was in charge of teaching any patients with ostomies or wounds the proper way to care for them. She also monitored them for any signs of problems or infections. By the time the ostomy nurse arrived, Jameson was fully awake from the anesthesia, and all things considered, was feeling pretty good.

After introducing herself to the three of us and going over some basics, she removed the surgical dressing so she could assess the ostomy. Jameson was eager to see the new part of him. He even asked for a mirror in order to obtain a closer look. No disgusting faces or derogatory remarks were made. He was sincerely interested in it, as was I. It was about the size of a half-dollar, and it had a nice healthy red color to it. Steve stole a brief look at it, but he rather quickly averted his gaze. When it came to all things medical, my husband was very weak-stomached. I was just glad that the initial introduction had gone so well for Jameson.

The number of visitors died down as the afternoon wore on, and Jameson seemed to rest comfortably. Late in the afternoon, we had an unexpected visit from Dr. Gunn's main surgical nurse. She said she was about to head home for the day and she just wanted to stop by and see how Jameson was doing. She told him he was looking good. She explained that she had been in the operating room assisting during both of his surgeries. She then stated that the mood in the OR that morning had been much different than the mood on Wednesday evening.

She went on to explain that on Wednesday the mood was very tense due to the critical nature of the surgery. She said her job was to hand Dr. Gunn the instruments as he needed them to perform the surgery. She somberly stated that when Jameson's abdomen had been fully opened and everything was in view, everyone in the operating room was aghast. She recalled that the situation looked so bad, she automatically began to cry. She then stopped what she was doing and immediately began to pray.

Jameson's condition had been so critical, the entire OR staff, including Dr. Gunn, didn't believe he would make it through the surgery. The nurse repeated that for the next few moments she felt that the best thing she could do for Jameson was to pray for God to please save him.

And miraculously, He did.

CHAPTER 12

May 7, 2001

Jameson was extremely well taken care of while in the intensive care unit. The nurses all provided excellent care.

They also continued to be very accommodating, throughout his stay, concerning the volume of visitors that were allowed in to see him.

His favorite nurse proved to be a big bear of a guy named Ralph. We discovered Ralph to be a very gentle, compassionate soul who was also a devoted father to his children, as well as his pets. Unfortunately, since Ralph was only helping out in the ICU, he was assigned to Jameson just once. He took special care to explain medications and procedures, and he would even quiz Jameson by asking him questions concerning the care he was receiving. Jameson impressed Steve and me, as well as Ralph, with, among other things, his knowledge of heparin and his overall willingness to learn.

The weekend had been relatively uneventful. Jameson had begun sitting up in the chair for short intervals and was taking walks within the ICU area. His abdominal incision originated just below his sternal (breastbone) area and ran down through his lower abdomen, so he remained quite sore. We all found it fascinating that his belly button had been removed during both surgeries and then replaced at the end of surgery. It looked to be in the exact same spot where God had originally put it. I guess Dr. Gunn really was a pretty good surgeon.

Speaking of Dr. Gunn, he did provide us with some welcome news over the weekend. He told us if Jameson continued to do as well as he had been doing, he would be transferred out of the ICU and into a regular room on Monday. I found this to be both exciting and a little unnerving. Exciting in the fact that it meant Jameson was improving and was that much closer to going home. It was unnerving because I realized Jameson wouldn't be receiving as much specialized care once he left the ICU. It was reassuring knowing that he had very competent nurses only a few steps away right outside his door.

Dr. Gunn had also made the comment to us that Jameson was a walking miracle. He explained that due to the condition of Jameson's small intestine during the initial surgery—the extent to which it was completely dead and already decaying—there should have been infection throughout his abdominal cavity. Jameson would also have been expected to have had infection throughout his entire bloodstream, a condition known as sepsis. There had not been one trace of infection; all blood cultures and other tests were completely clear.

My thoughts immediately recalled the words the OR nurse had spoken; she felt that the best thing she could do for Jameson was to pray for God to please save him. Then Dr. Gunn made another comment that I will never forget. He simply stated, "I'm not the one who saved Jameson's life." He then patted Jameson's arm and left the room.

Jameson eagerly awaited Monday. He had felt good during the weekend. Let me clarify. He had felt as good as a person could feel with a foot long incision running down the middle of his stomach, a portion of his small intestine peaking out through a second incision in his abdomen, a nasogastric tube in his nose and going down into his stomach, IVs in both arms, a second drainage tube inserted through a third abdominal incision, thick support stockings on both legs, alternating pressure boots on both feet and calves (to prevent blood clots post-surgery), and a large IV inserted into the jugular vein in his neck through which he received his total parenteral nutrition (TPN for short). The TPN was necessary to take care of Jameson's nutritional needs, since the short amount of small intestine which remained wouldn't adequately absorb enough nutrients from food to sustain him. But at least the Foley catheter had been removed.

Anyway, he was showing improvement, and he was ready to move into a regular hospital room. Dr. Gunn apparently liked to make early morning rounds, so Jameson and I both were anticipating being in a new room by lunchtime. We were mistaken.

The morning came and went. Lunchtime arrived, which had no real meaning to Jameson because he wasn't allowed to eat or drink anything, and passed. The afternoon crept along. We decided that Dr. Gunn had probably had a busy day and wouldn't make rounds until after office hours. Primetime television came on and still no Dr. Gunn. By this time I had decided, even if he did appear, I would prefer to wait until the following morning to change rooms. Jameson didn't share my sentiments. He wanted to move no matter what time Dr. Gunn showed up.

At ten o'clock, the wait was over. Dr. Gunn explained that he had been going nonstop all day, including an emergency surgery that he had just completed. He looked at Jameson and said, "Let's get you out of here."

Jameson was all smiles and in full agreement.

Even though it was close to shift change, the nurses were extremely accommodating to assist with the move. I continued to be a little apprehensive; I knew that on a busy surgical floor the nurses wouldn't be at our beck and call. But I was pleased that the move meant Jameson was progressing with his recovery.

Jameson was moved to a rather small room on the fourth floor. And I do mean small. It was barely big enough to hold the bed, a bedside table, and a small foldout couch. Jameson jokingly stated that he could almost lie in bed and touch the bathroom door.

The assigned nurse was pleasant, but it was obvious she wasn't thrilled with receiving a new patient right at the end of her shift (I wouldn't have been either). Steve had left the hospital a couple of hours earlier, so I phoned him to let him know Jameson's transfer did indeed take place. He was happy to hear it. One positive thing about the new little room—there was a shower in the bathroom! I wouldn't have to make the trek down the hallway to the public-patient shower anymore.

May 8, 2001

We both slept pretty well that first night; the nurses didn't come in as often as in the ICU. But I could foresee minor problems. The room was so small, there wasn't even enough room between Jameson's hospital bed and the fold-out sleeper sofa for me to get up when he needed something. I had to crawl down to the end and over the foot in order to get out of bed. And, if Jameson continued to have as many visitors as he had been having, there definitely wasn't going to be enough sitting space. Well, we would just have to adjust. Besides, did I mention that the bathroom had a shower?

During the course of the morning we met a few of the dayshift nurses. They were all nice and very busy. A little later in the morning, Carol, the fourth floor coordinator, had come to see us and to welcome Jameson back. I found it somewhat ironic that we were back on the fourth floor, the same floor that Jameson had been transferred to from the ER. Carol proceeded to tell Jameson that he had caused her to have a few more grey hairs during his first visit to the fourth floor.

She then told us that Jameson was going to be moved to a different room, a bigger room that she believed would be more comfortable for us. We were moved right down the hall to the very end of the hallway, room 439. The room was a very large, semi-private room that we were allowed to use as a private room.

With all of Jameson's visitors, we needed all the room we could get. And Steve and I, whichever one was spending the night, could sleep on a regular bed instead of a sleeper sofa or a reclining chair. But, there was one disappointment. As you've probably surmised, the bathroom did not have a shower.

Because of this, on Wednesday morning, I decided to go home and take a real shower. Steve had gone into work for half a day, and my parents had come to the hospital to stay with Jameson. This was the first time I had been home since taking him to the ER a week earlier.

The outside of the house looked the same as it always had. Even Jameson's pickup truck was parked in its usual spot in the driveway. As

I entered the house, I noticed how silent it was, almost reverent. Our sheltie, Abby, greeted me at the door. Boy, was I happy to see her, and she me.

After I had sat down and loved on Abby for a while, I decided to go upstairs and take a long shower in my own bathroom. As I climbed the stairs, thoughts flooded my mind. When I reached the top of the stairs, I was facing Ross's bedroom, and I had to chuckle. His room was as messy as always. As I turned to head into my room, I stopped.

There, at the far end of the hallway, directly in front of me, was Jameson's room. I felt drawn down the hallway and into his room, and I cried. I cried like a baby, hurt, inconsolable. His room was just as he had left it a week before. But the world had changed. I realized nothing would ever be like it was before.

Jameson had fallen in love with this room from the first time he saw it. It was actually a bonus room over the garage, but he claimed it for his bedroom. It was very spacious, and he had argued that since he was the older child, he should have the bigger room. Ross was not very happy, but Jameson's argument did have merit. Ross was later appeased by the combining of two smaller rooms to create one large room for him.

As I walked around the room, touching Jameson's belongings, I was determined to be strong and to think on the positive. Jameson would be returning to his home, to his room. Life may be different, but we were going to make it as normal as humanly possible. As I continued to cry, I silently prayed, *God, please bring my son home soon.*

I relished in the thought that he would be home soon. He was out of the ICU and into a regular hospital room. Dr. Gunn had previously told us that Jameson would probably remain in the hospital for about two weeks after he moved out of the intensive care. So, I thought, that meant only twelve or thirteen more days.

That was before the problems set in.

CHAPTER 13

May 14, 2001

Jameson had been making wonderful progress with his recovery. The removal of his NG tube had really helped his spirits. He would sit up in the chair most of the day. He also, although usually unwillingly, would ambulate down the hallway several times a day. The high point of his days was when he could use the opening in the back of his hospital gown to his advantage, which meant mooning visiting friends while ambulating down the hallway (since his room was located at the far end of the hallway, he could get away with public indecency).

He continued to have a lot of visitors. Three friends in particular proved to be mainstays during this time: Greg, who was a good friend from church, appeared on a regular basis; Kate, who had been Jameson's prom date just three days prior to his infamous ER visit, visited most days; and Wesley, Jameson's partner in crime at school, came to visit on a daily basis, sometimes he would show up twice in the same day. Aside from friends, other regular visitors included my parents, little brother Ross, and Brother Crist.

My parents graciously put their lives on hold in order to remain in Athens and help out in any way they could. Not only did they visit Jameson almost daily and take good care of our house and pets, most importantly they helped to keep Ross's life as normal as possible.

Speaking of Ross, I was impressed with his willingness to visit Jameson. Not only did he have a strong dislike for hospitals, but he and Jameson weren't the closest of brothers. Whenever Ross did visit, Jameson acted more like it was a nuisance for him to be there than being appreciative that he came. Ross was keenly aware of Jameson's attitude; still, he was usually agreeable to visit when encouraged to.

Besides his visitors, another thing that helped Jameson to remain in good spirits was the presence of his Nintendo 64 gaming system. We had obtained special permission from the hospital for this to be brought from home and setup in his room by the electrician on staff. Children that were long- term patients were sometimes allowed to bring electronics from home. Since Jameson was still a kid at heart, it just made sense for him to have something fun to help occupy his time (his friends enjoyed it, too).

Jameson also received visits from the high school faculty. One of the more memorable visits was from his English teacher, the one who assigned the research paper. She admitted to Jameson that when she found out about his medical emergency, and then remembered how she had responded to his question concerning being in the hospital, she cried in front of the entire class. She confessed that she had never cried during one of her classes before. She also said she would never again state that there was no acceptable excuse for turning in a late paper.

Another much-appreciated visit occurred when both the high school principal and the assistant principal showed up. They had just met with the Board of Education on Jameson's behalf. Because of his good academic standing, it had been decided that Jameson wouldn't have to makeup missed assignments or take final exams. The averages he had in each class at the time of his hospitalization would count as his final semester grades. He would also be allowed to pass the eleventh grade, even though he had an excessive number of days absent. He was one grateful young man.

Jameson had suffered only one real crisis since his release from the ICU. His biology class at school had scheduled to do their big dissection project on Thursday, May 10. He had been looking forward to this one event the entire semester. Since he was doing well, I had spoken with Dr.

Gunn about allowing Jameson to go out on pass for a couple of hours in order to participate in it. The answer was no.

Dr. Gunn explained that if anything were to happen to Jameson while he was off of the hospital grounds, the hospital would be held responsible. He also said he felt it would be too tiring for Jameson. We understood and accepted his reasoning, but Jameson certainly was disappointed that he was going to miss out on all the fun.

Despite the dissection disappointment, Jameson managed to have a great weekend, which also carried over into Monday. That Monday was a particularly special day. It marked day ten post-op, the number of days needed to be considered totally free from complications. There had been no complications so far from the last surgery.

That evening, for the first time, we all left Jameson to the mercy of the nurses so we could attend Ross's last band concert. He had decided not to be a part of the high school band, so this would probably be our last time to observe him as a trumpeter. If I might add, the band did a fantastic job that night.

After the concert, I arrived back at the hospital between nine-thirty and ten in the evening. As I walked into Jameson's room, he said something to the effect of, "That sure took a long time,"—then continued with—"I've got a fever."

I immediately got a sinking feeling. The end of day ten and he had a fever. I walked down the hallway and spoke with his nurse. She told me that Dr. Gunn had already been notified. The fever would be monitored, and we would just wait to see what happened.

Throughout the week, the cause of the fever was tried to be determined. Blood tests were drawn to rule out infections. Chest x-rays were taken to rule out pneumonia. Doppler studies were done to rule out blood clots in his legs. Nothing showed up. The fever remained an uninvited guest throughout the week. Because of his high fever, Jameson had also begun to grow weaker.

On Thursday night, a very upbeat friend of mine from work had come to visit. She also knew Jameson well because he had been a volunteer in the activities department where Christy was the director. Even her vivacious personality couldn't lift his spirits.

During Christy's visit, Jameson was unexpectedly taken downstairs to the x-ray department to have a CT scan of his abdomen. Dr. Gunn hoped to find something that would explain the mysterious fever. After Jameson returned from x-ray, we both settled into our respective beds for some much-needed rest. We were both exhausted—him physically, me emotionally.

The following morning I awoke early, between six and six-thirty. Since Jameson was still sleeping soundly and Dr. Gunn didn't make rounds until a little later in the morning, I decided to quickly run downstairs to the cafeteria and grab a biscuit to go. When I walked back into his room, Jameson was lying in bed crying.

I began to panic.

I hurried to his bedside. "What's wrong?" I frantically questioned.

"Where were you?" he sobbed. *"I've got to have another surgery!"* he cried.

"Oh, Jameson…when?" I could barely speak.

"Right now!" he again cried. *"They're going to be coming to get me. Dr. Gunn wanted to know where you were!"*

I tried to hold myself together and keep from crying in order to comfort and console him. Between crying, Jameson related to me that the CT scan had revealed that some of the previously questionable areas of the small intestine had indeed necrosed and would have to be removed immediately. I felt as though I had been kicked in the stomach; I couldn't imagine what Jameson was feeling.

I was feeling guilty for not being there with Jameson when he was told the news, but I was also feeling extremely upset at Dr. Gunn for unloading all of the news on Jameson while he was alone. He was a sixteen-year-old boy, for heaven's sake. Didn't Dr. Gunn think he would be a little upset by the news? He knew I had spent the night at the hospital! Couldn't he have waited five minutes for me to return to the room before he broke the news?

I didn't have time to feel guilt or anger right then. I had to get in touch with Steve and tell him what was happening, and I had to control my emotions while I spoke with him. I didn't want to upset Jameson any further, and I didn't want to panic Steve.

When I reached Steve, I immediately told him he needed to get to the hospital as quickly as possible, and then I gave him a brief explanation of the situation. I could tell he was also on the verge of falling apart, but he was able to pull himself together. I told him to ask my parents to get Ross off to school, and then for them to also come. Then I asked him to contact Brother Crist while he was driving to the hospital.

Then I asked him to please hurry.

CHAPTER 14

May 18, 2001

Jameson was taken into surgery for the third time on the morning of Friday the 18th. Steve had barely made it to the hospital in time to see him before he was taken down to the OR. My parents and Brother Crist all arrived shortly after he had been transported away.

The mood in the room was somber. We were all very upset and disappointed over the setback. The circumstances were very different from Jameson's previous surgery. That time, we were prepared for the surgery and were anticipating a positive outcome. Even the atmosphere in the packed waiting room had been light and positively-charged. In comparison, this surgery had been totally unexpected, and none of the five of us were very optimistic concerning the outcome.

The morning dragged on forever. The surgery seemed to be taking much longer than the previous two had. Worse yet, we hadn't received any updates from the operating room. Our conversations were merely idle small talk.

My mind kept wandering, and I could only think the worst. I also thought how, over the years, when I would hear about some tragedy or some life-altering event—someone's child had developed cancer, someone's son had been killed in a car accident, someone's little boy was missing—I would wonder how *I* would handle the situation. Would I fall apart? Would I act courageously and go on with my life? Would I withdraw into my own little cocoon? Would I blame God?

I emphasize that I had always just wondered about these things; I never, ever had wanted to experience any of those tragedies firsthand in order to test myself. And I had never wanted God to test me. But, that's exactly what I felt was taking place. I felt as though God was trying me to see how well I could deal with Jameson's illness—and I was not happy.

After the initial shock of everything had passed and the gravity of Jameson's entire situation had sunk into my being, I became very angry at God. I continued to thank Him for not taking Jameson from me and allowing him to live. But I was one mad mother, and my faith had definitely been shaken. I never asked God why Jameson had to have this happen to him; why he had to have his health taken away from him. But oh, did I demand to know why God hadn't intervened and prevented it from happening!

I mean, I knew God was capable of anything. Jameson should have died on the operating table; but he didn't. Jameson should have had a massive infection due to the extent of the necrosis to his intestine; but there was no sign of any infection. God had taken care of Jameson amazingly well thus far; but why did He even allow everything to happen in the first place? I just couldn't reconcile my feelings. And now, what was going to be the latest outcome of the most recent complication?

After what seemed like an eternity, Dr. Gunn came into the room. It was after 1:00 p.m. He began by saying that surgery had taken longer than he had anticipated, and that Jameson was doing well. He explained that because of the new areas of necrotic tissue, another foot of small intestine had to be removed.

That was disheartening news. After Jameson's initial surgery, when Dr. Gunn told us that Jameson had only approximately three feet of viable small intestine left, he also explained that that amount was right on the cusp of determining if Jameson would ever be able to survive without supplemental IV nutrition. We had been cautiously optimistic when there was three feet remaining, but now with only two—the odds were looking slim.

Also, because of the removal of so much more intestine, the ostomy had to be moved from the right side of the abdomen to the left. The remaining segment wasn't long enough to extend to the original opening. This meant a new incisional wound had been created, and another prime target for infection.

Time crept slowly for the remainder of the afternoon. Jameson remained in the recovery room for several hours—an unusually long time. We were routinely updated on his condition, each time being assured that he was stable and doing well. When he was finally returned to his room late in the afternoon, he looked pale, and completely worn-out.

Although Jameson's condition wasn't critical following this surgery, I felt as though the recovery time was going to take just as long, if not longer. His body was essentially starting all over in its healing process. This was the third major surgery in a two-week period. The third time his abdomen had been sliced open, including all of those strong abdominal muscles. The third time his internal organs had been handled and displaced and poked and prodded. The third time his small intestine had been cut in half, with one end positioned unnaturally outside of his body, while the other end remained suspended in animation deep within him.

Dr. Gunn had entered Jameson's abdominal cavity through the same incision each time. That also meant that he had completely removed Jameson's belly button each time, and then meticulously replaced it. I'd have to admit, he had done a fine job each time. The incision, although extremely big, was very clean and neat, and the belly button was in perfect position. We later learned that some people don't even have their belly buttons replaced after such extensive surgery. I was glad Jameson did.

He seemed to need even that little sense of normalcy.

CHAPTER 15

May 23, 2001

Jameson was almost a week post-op from his unexpected third surgery. I considered this surgery to be a major setback in his overall recovery, and it had definitely taken its toll on Jameson. His spirits were down, his physical strength appeared diminished, and his attitude was on the verge of "I don't care anymore." Aside from the fact that going through a third surgery had left him physically zapped, I think the idea of having to stay in the hospital longer than planned—including the fact that he would be spending his seventeenth birthday there—was causing some depression to creep in. It seemed as though Jameson was giving up, that everything that had happened was just more than he could deal with. I had gotten really concerned about him.

Because of my concern for his depressed state, I had contacted the therapist that Jameson had been working with prior to his hospitalization. I thought that since Jameson had established a trusting relationship with this counselor, it would be a good idea for him to come and visit. Maybe they could have an informal therapy session. I had called the office and briefly explained the situation, then had scheduled a time after office hours for the visit to take place.

Things didn't go quite as planned. To start with, Jameson had been having an exceptionally bad day all day. He didn't feel well at all, so that made him very grumpy. I had intentionally not told him that his therapist would be paying him a visit; I didn't want him knowing how concerned I was about his emotional state. Then, when the therapist arrived, he had his girlfriend in tow.

When they walked into his room, Jameson almost had a scowl on his face. He did not look happy. Jameson and the therapist exchanged greetings, and then the therapist introduced his girlfriend. Well, I'm no psychologist, but I did know that Jameson wouldn't open up about his feelings at all with a total stranger in the room. Besides, I felt uncomfortable being in there also, so I asked the girlfriend if she would mind keeping me company in the waiting room while the two guys visited. She caught on to my request well and followed me out of the room.

We had only been in the waiting room approximately fifteen minutes when the therapist walked in. He told me that although Jameson wasn't in a very talkative mood, he appeared to be doing okay. He then said if Jameson needed to come in to the office for a session after he was discharged from the hospital, just call and make an appointment.

I must admit, I was a bit taken aback. How could he have done Jameson much good in a mere fifteen-minute visit? Although I felt as though the visit had probably been a waste of time, I politely thanked him for coming. As it turned out, the visit wasn't such a waste of time for the therapist; I received a bill in the mail a few days later. He was well compensated for his time. I guess I was naive to think that he would have wanted to see Jameson out of sheer concern.

On top of everything else that had happened during the past week, nausea had become an almost constant companion to Jameson. It didn't matter if he was lying in bed, walking in the hallway, or sitting in a chair; he was plagued by nausea. The only thing that seemed to ease the nausea was a medication called Phenergan. It was a very common drug used to treat nausea occurring after surgery. It was most effective given intravenously, especially for people with short bowel syndrome since their bodies don't absorb a lot of things taken orally. As it turned out, Phenergan would be one of Jameson's best friends for a while.

Steve and I felt really badly for Jameson. He was so down in the dumps. There must be something we could do to help lift his spirits. We finally had an idea.

The hospital had a really nice covered patio area located adjacent to the cafeteria. We had taken Jameson out there a couple of times in order for him to just enjoy some fresh air. There was an access road that ran right behind the patio area.

We devised a plan to surprise Jameson with a visit from our sheltie, Abby. Jameson and Abby loved each other, and we felt it might do both of them good to see each other. Steve would pick Abby up after work and bring her to the hospital, parking inconspicuously on the access road. He would call me a few minutes before he arrived so I could have Jameson outside waiting. If we were caught with an unauthorized animal on the premises, we could possibly get in trouble. Oh well, that's a risk we would take.

Since Jameson's visit from his therapist hadn't quite gone as planned, I was hoping that this new plan we hatched would be a little more productive. Jameson had not been having a good day so far, so I was getting excited about Abby's visit. And, I must admit, I was looking forward to going out into the warm May afternoon.

After Steve called to let me know that he and Abby were on their way, I casually mentioned to Jameson that we should go out to the patio for a few minutes. I coaxed by saying what a nice day it was outside. He didn't seem to be buying into it. He said he didn't feel like going outside. I encouraged him by telling him it would make him feel better to get out of his room.

He persisted in saying he didn't want to go outside. I tried persuading him by offering to push him out there in a wheelchair instead of him walking. He continued to balk at the idea. I finally complained, "Jameson, I'm freezing in here. I've got to go outside for a few minutes to warm up. Come keep me company; it'll do you good." Begrudgingly, he finally agreed.

By the time we made it to the patio, I expected Steve to already be there. He wasn't. I pushed Jameson to the area farthest away from the cafeteria exit. I wanted our little visit to be unobserved. We sat there mostly in silence. Jameson wasn't in a talkative mood, and I didn't want to annoy him with idle chitchat. As I sat there relishing the warmth and fresh air, I kept wondering where Steve was. I knew I wouldn't be able to convince Jameson to stay outside much longer.

Finally, when Jameson had just begun complaining about wanting to go back to his room and get into bed, I saw Steve walking from the access road. He was leading Abby on her leash.

"Look who's here!" I exclaimed.

Jameson looked up and saw Steve and Abby coming toward him. A slight smile spread across his face.

"Hey, Abby," he said. "Come and see me."

Abby appeared excited to see him but nervous at the same time. She was in a strange place with all kinds of different smells. And Jameson was sitting in a wheelchair, not quite looking himself. Abby was used to Jameson immediately greeting her down on her level and showering her with affection. Also, Jameson had lost fifteen or twenty pounds during his stay in the hospital, and his voice was weak. It wasn't the strong, robust voice Abby was accustomed to hearing.

I walked over and lovingly greeted her, then lead her to Jameson's side. She still appeared uncertain, but once Jameson began to rub her and talk to her, she became more at ease. I questioned Steve as to why it had taken so long to get to the hospital. He explained that they had actually been there for several minutes, but upon arrival, there had been several occupied cars parked on the access road. He didn't think it would be a good idea to get out with Abby with so many witnesses present, so he drove around for a few minutes until the coast was clear.

The surprise of seeing Abby may have cheered Jameson for a brief period of time, but it was short lived. After only, at the most, ten minutes, Jameson was again requesting to go back to his room. He said he felt like he really needed to lie down. He thanked his daddy for bringing Abby to see him, and then he gave her one last pat on the head.

I told both Steve and Abby good-bye, and then I wheeled Jameson back to his sanctuary. As much as he hated being in the hospital, his room had become his haven. It almost took dynamite to even get him to walk a short distance in the hallway. And although I did whatever it took to present an optimistic, upbeat attitude, my spirits had also taken a nosedive.

I couldn't exactly pinpoint the reason for my feelings, but I knew I had to fight extremely hard to keep them under control. At times, I felt if only I could scream at the top of my lungs, or have an endless supply of plates that I could throw and smash to pieces; then I would feel much better. I was certain that I'd better not attempt either of the aforementioned activities for fear that I would be permanently escorted off of the premises by the hospital guards.

Other times, it took all I had just to fight back the tears and keep my composure. I refused to cry in front of Jameson; I felt as though he needed me to be strong. On a few occasions I had to quickly excuse myself from his room so I could find a place to be alone in order to have a meltdown. One such occasion occurred while Brother Crist was visiting.

Jameson had been having his ups and downs—both mentally and physically. Steve was fond of the phrase "two steps forward, one step backward." That pretty much summed up Jameson's life at that time. Late one afternoon, a lab technician had come into the room for the purpose of drawing blood. I knew Jameson had already had blood drawn that morning. He was already beginning to feel like a pincushion from all of the needle sticks he had endured, so I questioned the reason for having a second one drawn.

The technician politely explained that one of the earlier lab results had been abnormal, so the doctor had ordered for it to be repeated. For no apparent reason, I felt as though I was going to explode. I had to get out of the room. I excused myself for a few minutes and disappeared down the hallway into the vacant visitor's waiting room.

I sat down and attempted to talk myself into calming down. What was my problem? I had been pretty composed for three weeks; I couldn't start acting like a lunatic at this stage of the game. After sitting for a few minutes, I got up and began pacing around the small waiting area. Eventually, I felt I was calm enough to go back to Jameson's room.

As I approached the doorway, Brother Crist met me there. He asked if I was okay. I blubbered, "No." and then the waterworks started. I felt like an idiot, standing there crying my eyes out, and then my inner feelings just came pouring out.

I lamented about how I didn't know if Jameson or I could take many more setbacks: how it seemed that every time he began making progress, something would happen and set him back; how it broke my heart every time that happened; and, how unfair the whole situation was. It wasn't fair that all of this had happened to Jameson; that he hadn't deserved it. Then I felt embarrassed because I was standing in the middle of a hospital, spilling my guts to my pastor, and not in a very composed manner.

Brother Crist had stood quietly and allowed me to vent all of my feelings and emotions. He then put his arm around me and did what a loving pastor would do; he confirmed my feelings and told me he understood how hard the past few weeks had been. He didn't scold me for feeling as I did, but told me he would be surprised if I didn't have those feelings. He showed me compassion, understanding, and love. He didn't choose to condemn, but instead, he chose to acknowledge that I was human.

Far from perfect, but doing the best I could.

CHAPTER 16

May 26, 2001

We had been totally unsuccessful when it came to lifting Jameson's spirits. Really! Nothing we had tried in the past week had seemed to do any good. But I felt as though our newest scheme had to have some positive impact.

Today was Jameson's seventeenth birthday; fortunately, it fell on a Saturday. Though he had been depressed over the thought of spending it in the hospital, we were determined to make it at least a little better for him. We had planned a surprise party, complete with balloons, decorations, refreshments, and gag gifts. Jameson's friends—Wesley, Kate, and Greg—had been very instrumental in helping with the details and doing the invitations (and this time we had the hospital's permission for all of the visitors).

We had a difficult time deciding on whom to invite. We finally determined that the youth group from church and Jameson's friends from the high school swim team were the people he was closest to. These kids, along with a few close adult friends and Ross and my parents, made up the guest list.

As for refreshments, that was a much easier decision to reach. Jameson still wasn't allowed to eat; his intestinal tract was continuing to slowly heal. The only "food" that he was able to eat was popsicles.

Therefore, the only refreshments that were served at his party were popsicles. No birthday cake. No ice cream.

No party mints. Just an ice chest filled with assorted flavors of popsicles.

The party was scheduled for three o'clock on the covered patio. We had somehow managed to keep our mouths shut and keep the party a secret. Steve and I had given Jameson his gifts from us earlier in the day. They were items that he could look forward to using after he was home from the hospital, such as a new stereo system for his truck. We wanted to give the impression that we were celebrating his birthday, but not making a big deal out of it.

When it was time for the party, we had to be creative in order to get Jameson out of his room and down to the patio area. Wesley had come up with a plan. He called Jameson and told him he was coming to see him, and that he also had gotten a new car. He asked Jameson to come out to the patio area to see his car, and then he would go park in the parking deck and come back to keep him company for a while.

Jameson had hesitantly agreed to Wesley's request. He really had not wanted to leave the comfort of his bed, but he was curious to see the car. And besides, he couldn't tell Wesley no.

When we arrived outside at the patio—and everyone yelled "Happy Birthday!"—Jameson was truly shocked. He had the biggest grin on his face that I had seen in a while. His friends had done a really nice job of decorating, and everyone seemed to have a nice time. Approximately thirty-five people showed up for the big bash, most of whom were teenagers. There was also a table full of gifts.

Unfortunately, after only twenty minutes, Jameson told me he really needed to go back to bed. He said he didn't feel well at all, and he was very nauseated. Although he felt horrible, he still asked if his visitors could go back to his room with him. I knew I was probably going to be in trouble with the fourth-floor staff, but I agreed to his request anyway. After all, how many seventeenth birthdays would he have?

I announced to the party goers that Jameson needed to go back to his room, so we were moving the party there. I told them as soon as Jameson was settled and had been given his medicine, I would send for them. And that's what we did. After the nurse had given Jameson a dose of Phenergan to help relieve his nausea, I called Steve on his cell phone and gave the okay. Within a few minutes, friends, armed with gifts, invaded the room.

Not everyone that had initially been at the party came inside to continue the celebration, but there was a large group. The room was filled to capacity. Those of us who were overage sat in the lounge and visited. Thankfully, once Jameson was settled in bed and his medication had taken effect, he felt much better. The birthday celebration continued for another couple of hours. Gradually, as people began to leave, I felt satisfied that Jameson had truly enjoyed himself and that he was in a better frame of mind.

Finally, mission accomplished.

CHAPTER 17

June 5, 2001

Although Jameson's surprise party had been a success, the days following it were less than stellar. He continued to be plagued by nausea, and he stayed tired all of the time. The IV TPN that was being administered continually supposedly supplied all of his nutritional needs, but his weight didn't show any improvement. He just didn't appear very healthy.

Despite the fact that food was still a forbidden luxury, he had been allowed to start taking sips of certain juices such as apple, cranberry, and grape. Granted, that was a big accomplishment, but Jameson's craving for real food was getting the best of him. It had gotten to the point where when a commercial involving food would come on TV, he would turn the sound down and look away. In fact, he even was beginning to salivate at the sight of dog food. He was becoming a desperate young man.

Though the days were long, the nights proved to be even longer. Jameson had developed a severe case of insomnia; he would sleep for only short periods of time. The majority of the night was spent watching infomercials, primarily because there's not much to watch on television at three and four in the morning. We would lie awake in our respective beds and critique the products that were being hawked. The night nurses had made it a point to only come into the room when absolutely necessary; they didn't want to disturb Jameson in case he happened to be sleeping.

Another thing that contributed to Jameson's insomnia was that fact that he had become extremely hot-natured. His hospital bed was right beside the air conditioning unit, and the temperature was always set as low as possible. It didn't make any difference; he was always burning up. I, on the other hand, was always freezing, especially during the night. It didn't matter that it was summertime in Georgia, I always looked like I was ready for bedtime at the Arctic Circle. I slept in a long-sleeved turtleneck shirt, a sweat suit, and a pair of knee-high socks. My bedcovers consisted of a sheet and three blankets, two of which were always doubled. And I was still never warm.

However, despite everything that was going on, Jameson tried to make the best of a dismal situation. Somehow, his sense of humor managed to remain intact. No matter which friend was visiting, Jameson was always the consummate entertainer. As I mentioned previously, he had begun to drink certain juices and other clear liquids. He was supposed to be taking only sips of these liquids, but he would get carried away and drink cupfuls (he stayed constantly thirsty).

Because he continued to have a gastric drainage tube in place, each time he would drink something, the liquid would almost immediately drain back out of his stomach, through the tube and into the attached drainage bag. This phenomenon positively fascinated Jameson's friends, so he would perform this trick over and over again. The big excitement associated with this apparently was watching all of the different colors of fluids flowing through the tube.

Another form of entertainment that he provided was associated with his ostomy. This was not really something that could be performed on demand, but it was a rather frequent occurrence. Dependent upon the amount of gas that was built up in Jameson's digestive system, his ostomy would make noises.

One of those noises sounded remarkably like a duck quacking. This would always evoke a good laugh from who ever happened to be visiting.

Friday, June 1, had been a very important day in Jameson's recovery process. Throughout his hospital stay, he had been receiving his TPN through the IV in his neck. Since this was a temporary type of IV, it was required that he have a permanent IV surgically inserted in order to be allowed to go home.

A surgically implanted permanent IV line has a catheter that usually runs from the implant site into the superior vena cava of the heart. This allows large amounts of the IV nutrition to be infused and to spread throughout the body quickly and efficiently. Although there were several different types of medical devices available for this, we chose to have a portacath implanted.

A portacath is surgically inserted under the skin, usually in the upper chest beneath the collarbone. It is completely internal, unlike the other IV delivery devices, so swimming would not be a problem. That was key in our decision of which device to use.

A downside to the portacath was that a special needle had to be inserted through the skin and into the silicone bubble of the device for the TPN to be administered. The needle could be left in place for up to a week if Jameson wasn't participating in a swim meet and easily removed when he was required to be in the water. Truthfully, I didn't give him much choice as to which device he would receive. The one that allowed him the best chance to continue on with his life as he once knew it was the *only* choice as far as I was concerned.

He had his port inserted on the left side of his chest on Friday afternoon, six days after his seventeenth birthday. What I had explained to Jameson and Steve as a fairly simple procedure turned out to be a stroll through hell. Jameson was in more pain from that simple procedure than he had been in from any of the other major surgeries. Nothing seemed to ease the discomfort.

He received morphine as often as possible, but it really didn't seem to help. Steve had originally planned on staying that night at the hospital while I went home; I couldn't leave Jameson in such agony. I didn't know what I could do to help relieve his discomfort, but I knew I had to be there for him. Needless to say, it was a long, agonizing night.

To top it off, Jameson's abdominal drainage tube became disconnected not once, but twice during the middle of the night. That meant his entire bed linens had to be completely changed, two different times. Making him change positions caused him excruciating pain. That one night was the only time I had ever seen him cry from the pain; it truly broke my heart.

Things were somewhat better with the light of day. Jameson was still in pain, but it wasn't as severe. And since the port was in place, the prospect of going home could become a reality. Since his last major surgery two weeks before, Jameson's recovery seemed to have slowed down. He tired more easily, his enthusiasm for ambulating in the hallway was nil, he was sleeping horribly at night, and he had begun to have the shakes. Despite everything, we felt if we could only get him home, everything would be alright.

Speaking of Jameson's homecoming, Steve and I had been discussing it for the past few days. We were both very eager to get him home, but there was some anxiety also. I had often wondered over the years why God had led me into the field of nursing, because honestly, it was not a career that I had ever wanted to pursue. During Jameson's stay in the hospital, God had finally enlightened me that Jameson would require medical care from now on; I was a medical care provider. Aha! It finally made sense. But I was still nervous. I had taken care of a lot of patients over the years, but none of them were my son. I hoped I could handle the task at hand.

And Steve, he was so anxious to just get Jameson back home. He wanted to make certain that everything was just right for his homecoming. He was especially concerned about how weak Jameson had become, and whether he would be able to make it up the stairs to his bedroom. Jameson slept in a water bed, and we had already decided that would be too difficult for him to get in and out of. We thought the best solution would be for Jameson to temporarily sleep in the guest bedroom. The bed had a comfortable mattress, and the room itself was in close proximity to our bedroom.

Steve continued to worry about the stairway. So as Jameson's dismissal had drawn closer, he had asked me if I thought we should rent a hospital bed and place it downstairs in the living room so Jameson wouldn't have to climb the stairs.

I immediately snapped back at him, "No! We are not going to get him a hospital bed! He is not an invalid!" Poor Steve, his only response was, "Okay."

I did apologize for my abruptness. I knew we both were just trying to do what was best for Jameson. And we both were terribly frightened of the unknown.

As the weekend had passed, unfortunately Sunday nor Monday were very good days, either. Jameson just didn't feel real well, and the shaking and sleeplessness had actually worsened. Neither doctor was really sure about what was going on. I was afraid our prospects of going home were lessening again. Steve stayed at the hospital on Monday night, and I went home to my bed. One of us had stayed at the hospital with Jameson every night, and though he complained about it, I think he was actually grateful.

The phone rang at home early Tuesday morning; it was Jameson. He announced that he was being discharged. Well thank goodness! Five weeks after the nightmare had begun, our young man would finally return home and to his life.

Those had to have been the longest, most draining five weeks of our lives. It was impossible to put into words all of the different emotions that had come into play over that period of time, but the emotion at that moment was extreme thankfulness—thankfulness that my son wasn't taken from us, thankfulness that his spirit was unable to be broken—and now thankfulness that our family would be back together and whole once again.

Oh, the road back would be a long, hard one. There would be more surgeries, more hospital visits, more bad days, more doubt and hurt and confusion. But for that one day, that Tuesday afternoon, all *was* well. Our son was completing his long journey home.

PART III

THE TRANSITION

CHAPTER 18

June 2001

Bringing Jameson home from the hospital was both wonderful and terrifying, all at the same time. Ross made a "Welcome Home" poster and had placed it in the back of Jameson's truck so he could see it as we pulled into the driveway. Abby was thrilled when the three of us walked in the door together. Jameson went straight to the sofa and sat down, and Abby was immediately right up there beside him.

Steve and I had both felt that if we could just get him home, everything would be better. We were only kidding ourselves. There were no nurses to bring him pain or nausea medicine, or administer his TPN, or take care of his ostomy, or monitor him for infections, or assist him in climbing those damn stairs. As a nurse, I had all of the training and knowledge that was needed to give my son the best medical care. But taking care of *my* son would be different from taking care of other patients, and I truly felt inadequate. I guess actually scared would be a better description.

Jameson was extremely relieved to be home, although his first few weeks back didn't go exactly smoothly. Yes, I did feel a pang of guilt the first time he climbed the staircase, but he did an excellent job. And, Steve and I both knew that exercise would enable him to regain his strength and build up his muscle tone.

Lying in a bed for five weeks, plus going through three major surgeries in that same amount of time, really took the wind out of his sails!

Due to his weakened state, and the fact that the nausea would not go away, Jameson was very opposed to any official exercise, but Steve would make him walk around the yard anyway. That is, until we had a new home health nurse come to visit one Saturday. The nurses from our original home health agency were not very proficient with taking care of Jameson's central IV line, nor were they well-educated with any aspects of TPN. After making a couple of phone calls, our insurance company provided us with an agency that specialized in IVs—all types of IVs.

The nurse that visited on that particular Saturday was an angel named Pam. She and Jameson connected immediately. After doing her assessment and taking his vital signs, she told us that Jameson appeared to be extremely dehydrated. She contacted the on-call physician and received orders to infuse additional IV fluids in order to combat the dehydration.

Steve and I both felt awful. I wondered how I could be a nurse and have neglected to recognize that important fact. Steve really felt bad because he had been making Jameson walk around outside in the summer heat. Pam consoled both of us and assured us that we were not the problem. Jameson was losing too much fluid through his gastric drainage tube. He needed to really decrease the amount of fluids he drank. We later learned that dehydration was the number one cause of hospitalizations for people with short bowel syndrome. We all gradually, over time, gained knowledge and wisdom.

Along with the fluids Jameson had been losing, he had also lost more weight, which was not uncommon. He was very thin. His ribs and pelvic bones protruded, and his arms and legs resembled a stick figure. Steve and I realized that he was skinny, but we didn't worry over it too much because we knew before long the TPN would enable him to regain his weight.

One afternoon, Jameson began crying. He told us, "I looked at myself in the mirror, and I don't even look like me anymore!" He was inconsolable. We felt horrible for him. We knew there was really nothing we could say at the moment that would help, so we just sat with him and let him cry for a while. He appeared to feel a little better afterwards, but we realized that we needed some advice on how to best help him.

A few days later, I contacted Dr. Gunn to inquire about Jameson receiving outpatient physical therapy. I explained that he simply wasn't regaining his strength and that he had no stamina. Dr. Gunn recommended that instead of physical therapy, he felt Jameson would benefit from working with a personal trainer. That sounded like a great idea to us. We at once began making phone calls to various gyms in order to locate a trainer that also had experience working with medically compromised individuals.

In the meantime, only two short weeks after Jameson's release from the hospital, we experienced the first, of what would be numerous, IV line infections. And they could be vicious. The first symptom would usually be a headache, followed by chills and an abnormally high fever (the norm for Jameson was 104-105 degrees), and increased nausea. When the first one hit, I had no idea what was happening, other than there had to be an infection somewhere. I immediately began to worry that something had gone wrong internally.

I phoned Dr. Wells. Since he suspected an infection of the IV central line, he in turn contacted our home health agency and had a nurse visit and obtain blood cultures. These cultures would indeed verify if the infection was in the IV line, and would subsequently identify the type of infection. Identification of the infection type was crucial in knowing which antibiotic would effectively eradicate it. Unfortunately, the cultures usually required 48-72 hours to grow completely.

Since Jameson was a pretty sick kid, Dr. Wells wanted to start him on some type of antibiotic right away, at least to fight off any secondary infection. He actually came to our house on his way home from work and gave Jameson an antibiotic injection. We were startled to see him standing at our front door when he arrived, but it was so very comforting to know he cared that much about Jameson's welfare.

Due to the severity of the infection, it took the culture less than twenty-four hours to grow. We were able to begin an IV antibiotic the very next day. We were fortunately able to keep Jameson out of the hospital and administer IV antibiotics at home on numerous occasions, thanks to my nursing skills. The antibiotics would usually begin clearing up the infections rather quickly. But the added IV time would keep us prisoners in our house, despite the fact that IV administration had improved by leaps and bounds in recent years.

When you think of IVs, the image of a large, noisy pump attached to a rolling pole comes to mind. That is not the case for long-term, at-home IV therapy. Jameson's pump was about the size of a 4x6 photo, only thicker. The pump and the bag of TPN solution both fit inside a specially designed backpack; all that could be seen was a small section of IV tubing. The sound of the pump was barely audible, only a soft whir.

None of that mattered to Jameson; he didn't like to go anywhere while he was receiving his TPN. The TPN solution itself had to infuse over eighteen hours, which left only six hours of "free time." When antibiotics were thrown into the mix, the free time dwindled down to only two or three hours. While Jameson was recovering from his first infection, we had located a personal trainer for him.

Tim was a perfect fit. He had worked with several clients requiring specialized fitness programs due to medical issues. He was young, outgoing, and tough but compassionate. His gym was small and personal, not the type of place where people went to be seen and flaunt their physiques.

Jameson was very reluctant to go, and I was reluctant to go and leave him, but we both made it through on his first day. He usually worked out three days a week, and he worked hard. Some days he really didn't feel well, but he went anyway. Other days his workout was so strenuous, I had to pull over on the drive home so he could throw up. But his time in the gym paid off. His strength and endurance increased, and he slowly began to regain some of his confidence back.

CHAPTER 19

July 2001

Due to the upheaval of our lives during the past two months, Steve and I decided to postpone the entire People to People trip and reschedule it for the next summer. Unfortunately, this decision did not sit well with Ross; it was a major disappointment, and it made him extremely angry and unhappy. He repeatedly told us how unfair we were being to him; he emphasized that it wasn't *his* fault that Jameson had gotten sick. Fortunately, a friend in Pennsylvania invited him to come for a long visit. Thankfully the chance to see old friends did help to lift his spirits.

While Ross was away on his trip, Jameson, Steve, and I made the two-hour trip to Augusta to visit Dr. Martindale, the physician Dr. Gunn had consulted with following the initial surgery. He would be performing the intestinal anastomosis on Jameson in a couple of months. In layman's terms, he would reconnect the small intestine to the large intestine, therefore, doing away with the ostomy. Dr. Martindale was a leading authority in the gastrointestinal field, and an expert on small bowel syndrome. I think we all fell in love with him at that initial meeting. He made us feel very at ease. Also, he was extremely friendly and down-to-earth for someone who was so intelligent.

Before we left Dr. Martindale, we asked him when Jameson would be allowed to eat again; he looked surprised. We explained that Jameson hadn't eaten anything since his initial surgery on May 2 in order for his intestine to rest and heal optimally.

Dr. Martindale blurted out, "Give that boy some food! Let him eat small amounts of whatever he wants, as long as it doesn't make him sick." Of course, the nutritionist made some clarifications, and did set a few boundaries, concerning the foods that Jameson was allowed to eat. The important thing was Jameson could eat!

The three of us were so excited. We had been waiting on this day for weeks. On the ride home, we asked Jameson several times if he wanted to stop and get something to eat. He declined each time, saying he would try eating when we got home.

When we did arrive home, Jameson made his food request. After weeks of not being allowed to eat, the first thing he had the taste for was a dill pickle. I laughed and asked him if he was pregnant. He replied that he wanted to start off eating slowly, and a pickle just really sounded good. So, a pickle it was!

Due to his ever present nausea, Jameson very gradually began eating again. He learned which foods he could tolerate well, and which ones just didn't agree with him. Since his discharge from the hospital, he also continued to be plagued with insomnia. Because of his inability to maneuver well in his own water bed, Jameson continued to sleep in the spare bedroom, which was across the hall from our master bedroom. Because Steve and I had become so paranoid about everything, we used walkie-talkies as a means for Jameson to call if he needed us during the night.

Some nights when he couldn't sleep, he would call me into the room. We would sometimes just talk to pass the time. Other times I would doze as he lay awake. I think it was just comforting for him to have someone in the room. On the nights we talked, our conversations covered a multitude of topics: past experiences, what the future might hold, religion. Jameson could make me feel extremely guilty. While I couldn't help holding a grudge against God, Jameson praised Him for allowing him to live. He also rarely felt sorry for himself, where as I wallowed in self-pity more than I should.

Another hurdle that had to be overcome was Jameson's fear of socializing. Although his confidence was steadily improving, he still had quite a ways to go. He was reluctant to attend gatherings at friends' homes for fear of becoming sick, having his ostomy pouch come loose, or having his drainage tube leak. He was also still very thin, which made him self-conscious. With the support of his friends, and our constant encouragement, he finally began visiting people outside of our home. And he found that he enjoyed himself.

He learned that his friends saw him as the same old Jameson he had always been. They didn't care that his life had taken a detour; they knew he was still the same friend that joked around and made them laugh. Jameson did, however, develop a catchphrase that both entertained his friends and suckered his family into catering to his every whim. Whenever he wanted something in particular or needed to get his way, he would pout his lips and say in the most serious little boy voice, "I almost died!"

I know. You're thinking, "How could that be entertaining in the least bit?" Trust me. You had to have been there. It worked like a charm, for quite a while. As his health improved, the phrase began to lose its power. But in those early days, when the hurt was fresh and raw, we had to learn to laugh to keep from crying. Lightheartedness helped us keep our sanity.

After getting Jameson back into the social scene, we had to convince him to begin driving again. It's not that Steve nor I minded transporting him to wherever he wanted or needed to go; we really didn't. We felt that driving was an important step towards him regaining some of his independence.

It so happened that a close friend was having a family dinner in celebration of her seventeenth birthday, and she really wanted Jameson to be a part of it. After some coaxing, he accepted the invitation. Since Ashley's house was only a few miles away, Steve and I worked out a deal with him. I would drive him to her house, and Steve would drive Jameson's truck there. If he felt well enough after dinner, Jameson could drive himself home. If not, we would retrieve him and his truck.

A couple of hours after we had taken him to Ashley's, Jameson pulled into our driveway. He was almost giddy. He said he had forgotten how good it felt to be behind the wheel of a car and actually driving. It was wonderful to see him in such a good mood. I happily put away my chauffeur's license, at least for a few weeks.

Jameson ended up back in the hospital at the end of the month. We had decided to go to Florida and spend a few days at the beach—sort of a family getaway. We stopped by my parents' house on the way to leave Abby. While there, Jameson discovered that his ostomy bag had filled with blood. I tried not to show panic, but I felt a little frantic. We ushered Abby back into the minivan, and hurriedly headed back to Athens.

When I spoke with Dr. Wells, he instructed us to go straight to the hospital. He called the hospital and left orders for Jameson to be a direct admission (which meant he wouldn't have to be first seen in the ER) . Jameson wasn't really in pain, but I could tell he was concerned; we all were.

The following morning Jameson had an endoscopy performed in order to take a look at the lining of his stomach and upper small intestine. Following the procedure, the GI doctor explained to Steve and me that the portion of the intestine at the ostomy site had become severely ulcerated. This would require removal of more of the small intestine. I knew every inch of intestine that was removed meant it would be more difficult for Jameson to function without TPN.

When I openly voiced my disappointment concerning the loss of yet more intestine, the doctor matter-of-factly replied, "It doesn't really matter how much intestine he's left with. He's going to be on TPN for the rest of his life anyway."

All I could do was sit there and stare at him. I knew if I opened my mouth to say anything, I would start crying. My silence didn't make any difference; I began crying anyway. I couldn't believe he was so blunt and unsympathetic. No matter what he said, we wouldn't lose hope that one day Jameson might be able to live a healthy life, free of TPN. Needless to say, that doctor was forever blacklisted from our lives.

CHAPTER 20

August 2001

Due to the unexpected bleeding that Jameson had begun experiencing, Dr. Martindale decided to perform the reconnection surgery earlier than originally planned. The amount of bleeding had significantly decreased, but the doctor thought it was best to remove the area of the damaged intestine as soon as possible. The first available day was the third, one week before school started back.

My wish was for Jameson's senior year of high school to be as normal as possible. I had wanted him to be able to attend school for the first few weeks in order to get settled in, and then have his surgery toward the end of September. I also wanted Ross's transition into high school to go smoothly; I had hoped to give him extra attention for the first few weeks. Looked like my wishes and hopes were going to be squashed.

Well, at least Jameson's surgery would be over with. He looked so forward to being rid of his ostomy and its drainage bag; in his mind, the sooner the better.

The surgery went well. It was long, approximately eight hours, but Dr. Martindale had explained that it would be extensive and take most of the day. Initially, there had been some concern as to whether a small muscular ring, known as the ileocecal valve, would be salvageable. This muscle is located at the junction of the small and large intestine. It blocks wastes from backing up into the small intestine, and it regulates the emptying of digested food materials from the small intestine into the large intestine.

Dr. Martindale had explained that Jameson could function without this valve, but it would make his life much easier if it remained intact and functioning. Steve was worried to death that it couldn't be saved. In the middle of the surgery, Dr. Martindale himself came to the waiting room to let us know that everything was going well. He made our day when he told us the ileocecal valve appeared to be in good shape and would remain a vital part of Jameson's digestive tract. I thought Steve was going to hug him right there on the spot!

It was great having the surgery over and done with, but the recovery was agony. Not that Jameson was in severe pain, but being two hours away from home made everything more difficult. None of his friends made the two hour trek, so the days were long and boring. Even my parents were able to make only a couple of visits. Steve wasn't able to take much time off from work. We did arrange it so I could be with Ross his first day of high school; that was a top priority for me. I felt as though he needed little reminders that he was just as important to us as Jameson; Jameson's situation simply required a lot of our time and energy.

The fact that Jameson's GI system was once again all connected and in full working order was a miracle, but even miracles can take some getting used to. His GI tract was working overtime. Short bowel syndrome means just what it sounds like—the intestinal tract is severely shortened in length; therefore, foods and liquids pass through at a much more rapid rate. Once Jameson was allowed to eat, he was going to the bathroom eighteen to twenty times a day. That alone made sleeping at night, or any time, virtually impossible. I couldn't help but think that maybe he would've been better off to have kept his ostomy, with its little duck noises.

To add insult to injury, when he would be sleeping, residents and interns would sometimes make rounds at four or five in the morning. This made Jameson and me both very grumpy, but we had to deal with it. After all, he was a patient at one of the top teaching hospitals in the state; we needed to be thankful for the opportunity instead of grumbling.

After spending only ten days in the hospital, we were headed home. I had to assure Steve that it wasn't necessary for him to take a day off from work; I could deliver Jameson home safely, without any assistance. The trip was uneventful. We even made a stop at his favorite restaurant, although not to eat. Dr. Martindale had warned Jameson to always know where the bathroom was located, wherever he went. That proved to be very sound advice.

CHAPTER 21

September 2001

Jameson spent most of his days napping on the couch and watching TV. He was sleeping better at night, but he awakened very early. I usually found him already on the sofa when I went downstairs each morning. For some reason, he could go back to sleep once he got settled in the family room. His sleeping schedule made it difficult for me to do household chores; I revised my schedule to fit his.

Until Dr. Martindale released him to go back to school, Jameson was considered a homebound student. He was assigned a tutor. She brought him his weekly class assignments and was supposed to assist him with them as needed. She also turned them back in for him. His semester classes included calculus and a speech class. We thought he would need to drop his speech class, since it's a little difficult to present a speech when you're not in class, but his teacher allowed him to videotape them. He turned them in once he returned to school.

The tudor was a nice older lady but not very reliable. Some weeks she was late bringing the assignments, so Jameson had to rush to complete them on time. And she did not help with any subjects, particularly math. Therefore, Steve inherited the role of calculus tutor, and he did a fine job. He and Jameson worked hard and spent many hours mastering calculus.

Meanwhile, I inherited the role of sucker. During Jameson's first hospitalization, he began asking for a puppy. Because I felt sorry for him, in a moment of weakness, I agreed to his request. I knew better than to even entertain the thought of buying a puppy; I had my hands full enough with taking care of Jameson. Luckily, Ross seemed to be adapting well to ninth grade. Because of his smaller stature, I had worried about him being bullied by upperclassmen; but so far, so good. He hadn't been shoved into any lockers or humiliated in any other way.

So, of course, we bought a puppy. Jameson had decided on a cairn terrier (like Toto in *The Wizard of Oz*) . I located a breeder, Jameson chose the puppy he wanted, and we added a new member to our family. He named him Otto, and he was wild—cute, but wild. It went without saying, but then I truly had my hands full! Training a puppy took a lot of time, which I didn't have an excess of. Both Jameson and Ross were more than happy to play with Otto, but not so much help with training or cleaning up after him.

On the morning of September 11, when our country changed, Jameson was sleeping peacefully on the couch. I was working in the kitchen. A neighbor phoned and asked if I was watching TV. I replied that I wasn't because Jameson was sleeping. She told me to go turn on the television; she stated we were under attack. She hurriedly explained that a plane had flown into the World Trade Center, and there had been an explosion. We quickly said our good-byes and hung up.

As I turned on my television and took a step back, a plane flew into the second tower, and a fireball erupted. I couldn't believe what I had just witnessed! As I stood there watching, I heard Jameson's voice behind me ask, "What's going on?"

I turned around and apologized for waking him, then explained what was happening. I sat down on the couch at his feet, and together we watched the horror unfold. After a while, Jameson fell back asleep. Shortly thereafter, when I simply couldn't watch it any longer, I turned the television off and continued on with my life, feeling somewhat guilty that I was able to do just that.

Jameson had steadily gained weight and was beginning to look healthy again. The infusion rate on his TPN was increased, so he was hooked up to the IV a fewer number of hours. On good days, his trips to the bathroom were even less than the normal fifteen to eighteen. His appetite had also slowly increased, so he was eating more normally.

He had even discovered a college he was interested in attending after graduation. His senior class had attended a large college fair held in downtown Athens. Since Jameson was nervous about riding with a bus full of his peers (due to his frequent nausea and bathroom urgency), I persuaded him to allow me to take him there. I promised I wouldn't hover; I'd let him leisurely look around.

I was happy to get him to the fair. Prior to his illness, he had no desire to attend college. During his recuperation, he decided he would like to be a marine biologist. I realized training for that career might be a little tricky, considering he would have to be in the water quite a bit. Not a simple task for someone with a permanent IV in place. I did, however, believe in the old saying, "Where there's a will, there's a way."

He walked around the large convention center for a short while, and then announced he was done. He had gathered literature from a small college in St. Petersburg, Florida named Eckerd College. Ironically, I had recently read an article about that very college in an education magazine. But, wasn't St. Petersburg located in a foreign country? Oh no, wait, that's just how faraway it seemed it was. Well, I would worry about distance when the time came. I was just thrilled that Jameson was showing a true interest in college.

Another thing that had his interest was a big music festival in Atlanta. He had been looking forward to it before he became ill, and he was still excited about it. Steve and I thought it was a bad idea, but Jameson was determined to go. He wasn't well enough to attend school, but he thought he could hold out to go to an all-day music festival, in the Georgia heat.

A plan was devised. Wesley, Jameson's guardian angel friend, would drive them to the outskirts of Atlanta, where they would board a commuter train to transport them and thousands of their closest friends to the festival site. Did I mention that Ross also went? He and

Jameson had very little to do with each other, but he had been invited to tag along since there was an extra ticket available. We made Jameson promise that he would stay in the shade as much as possible and drink enough water to feel his eyeballs floating; dehydration was not allowed. We also made both him and Wesley promise that they would keep an eye on Ross and not lose him.

After the trio left, neither Steve nor I could stand to stay home and worry about Jameson all day (and fear Ross becoming lost). We knew we were terrible parents for letting him go, but we also knew we couldn't continue to baby him. We spent the day riding around, enjoying the countryside, and touring a little historic town. I'm not quite sure how we resisted the urge to call Jameson's cell phone every five minutes, but we did. That's not to say we didn't check ours every ten minutes just to make certain we hadn't missed a call from him.

The boys, all three of them, arrived back home around ten that night. They all agreed it had been a long day but a fun one. Jameson had acquainted himself several times with the portable potties and had also thrown up a few times. He commented that he was really tired, but he had proved that he could do it—he had enough stamina to hold out all day.

CHAPTER 22

October 2001

On the first day of October, Jameson made his triumphant return to school. Per Dr. Martindale's orders, he attended only half days for the first month. We met with his teachers and the principal to discuss ways in which his new health needs could be met.

Everyone was very understanding and accommodating. He was given a hall pass for the entire year and told that anytime he needed to go to the restroom, he could simply get up and walk out of class. It was also agreed that anytime he began feeling sick or extremely bad, he was allowed to sign out at the office and go home. I would always be notified that he had left the school premises.

Once Jameson got back into the routine and rhythm of school, life seemed more normal. He even attended a few football games while infusing his TPN. He attended swim practice a couple of days a week, and he participated in each swim meet. Although he was disappointed that his time scores were slower than previously, he was happy to be back with his teammates. He even displayed his surgery scars with a sense of pride, knowing he had beaten the odds. Once he displayed his sense of humor, and his team spirit, by highlighting his scars with royal blue body paint, one of the school colors.

Ross's world appeared to be on a pretty even keel. He had been a member of Boy Scouts forever; their meetings and activities kept him comfortably busy. He also appeared to be adjusting well to high school. His grades were good, his complaints minimal, and his group of friends was expanding. We were slowly becoming acquainted with his new friends, although sometimes in rather unique ways.

Since Jameson was feeling confident enough to be left alone at home for brief periods, Steve and I would occasionally venture out for a little together time. While talking with Jameson upon our arrival home one Saturday night, we realized we hadn't seen Ross anywhere. When we asked where he was, Jameson told us that one of his new friends had come over a little earlier. When we inquired as to their whereabouts, Jameson answered, "Up in a tree; they are so weird." Steve and I both looked at him and asked, "They're where?"

Jameson pointed us to the specific tree. We went outside and, sure enough, there was Ross, and a boy we had never seen before, sitting on a large branch up in the tree. When asked why they were in the tree, Ross nonchalantly informed us that they had been bored, so they decided to climb a tree. I told them to be careful climbing back down, and Steve and I went back inside, both of us shaking our heads. Our younger son definitely marched to the beat of a different drum.

The next social hurdle for Jameson had been the school homecoming dance. After I annoyed him enough, he said he would consider going, but he felt awkward about asking someone on a date; he didn't feel he was ready for dating. I recommended he ask one of his friends; that way, it wouldn't really be a date, just two friends enjoying each other's company for the evening.

Jameson was still reluctant, so I sweetened the pot. I told him if he would go, I would rent him a sports car for the evening. That was the bargaining chip I needed to persuade him to go. After making several phone calls, I found what I was looking for. So what if the car had to be picked up in Atlanta and then delivered back to Atlanta (only a three hour drive round trip). And it had to be a two-day rental. And I didn't tell Steve until *after* I had made the reservation.

The night of the dance, Jameson and his date looked stunning, especially while riding in a silver Mercedes convertible. Steve initially thought I was crazy for paying what I did to rent the car, but having the fun of driving it for part of the weekend helped to soften his opinion. A good time was had by all.

The following weekend, Jameson and I took a road trip down to Florida in order to tour Eckerd College. He had his mind made up that he was going to attend there. The drive wasn't bad; it took eight hours, door to door.

He was very excited as we pulled onto the campus. The school's enrollment was only fifteen hundred students, so the campus was small. In typical Florida fashion, it was dotted with palm trees. It also sat on a small bay.

After taking a tour, we checked in at the motel where we were staying. It was a rather old, no frills motel, but that didn't really matter. What did matter was that we were right on the beach—the beautiful, white sands of the Gulf of Mexico. Our beach trip in July had been thwarted, but not this time.

We had a very nice weekend; the best part was that we enjoyed each other's company. We took walks along the water's edge, ate seafood while watching the sun set over the ocean, and discussed the future—Jameson's future. In a few short months, I was fairly certain that he would be moving to the college on the bay. I would be sad to let him go, but at the same time, happy. He would venture out on his own and prove to everyone, especially himself, that he could make it.

CHAPTER 23

November 2001

Jameson had begun attending school full time, and I had returned to work. Although it felt so good to be out of the house and once again be a member of society, I continued to be an emotional basket case. In the middle of any given activity—whether it was cleaning the house, making phone calls at work, or just driving down the road—I would burst into tears. I had no control over it. I had quite a few little talks with myself on those occasions. My advice would usually be, "Get a hold of yourself; you can do this" or "This too shall pass."

I also couldn't control my anger at God; I was still so upset with Him for allowing Jameson's health to be taken away. I questioned over and over why He hadn't prevented it. I think I was so mad because I knew God could have prevented everything, but He chose not to intervene.

To add insult to injury, each time Jameson seemed to be making a little headway, he would become ill again. I became convinced that it was me bringing him bad luck because of my fractured relationship with God. I even got to the point that I was afraid to pray for Jameson's comfort and health; my prayers always seemed to backfire.

One night, after Jameson began running yet another fever, Steve and I were at the kitchen table; I was preparing the TPN.

Suddenly, I became so angry; I began throwing IV supplies across the table. I then snatched up a chair from under the table and threw it into the wall and the adjoining window. I then screamed at God. "Jameson is not Job! Just leave him alone!"

I'm certain my family was convinced that I had turned into a raving lunatic. I was embarrassed by my outburst, but I couldn't contain my emotions. As a mother, I felt helpless, and somewhat distraught. I wanted something I knew I could never have. I wanted my son back the way he was, his health fully restored.

Aside from the normal rough patches along the way, November was a time of praise. The Thanksgiving holidays had a special meaning for us because Jameson was alive and able to take part in it. We indulged in two separate feasts—one with my family and one with Steve's. Jameson made a list requesting all of the foods he wanted cooked for Thanksgiving Day. Of course, his eyes turned out to be bigger than his stomach, but the rest of us didn't mind helping him eat all of the food.

Another "Thanksgiving" occurred when Dr. Martindale removed the gastric drainage tube that had been a part of Jameson's anatomy since May. The tube had basically been clamped off for several months. It was only opened to drain when Jameson became extremely nauseated or when his stomach felt really full. The G-tube had become sort of a release valve.

The tube had also become a type of security blanket for Jameson. Even though he rarely used it anymore, he didn't want it removed. Up until the time Dr. Martindale did remove it, Jameson continued to plead his case to keep it. I viewed its removal as one less thing to have to worry about. Jameson eventually viewed its absence as one step closer towards obtaining independence.

PHOTOS

Jameson, age 5, and Ross, age 2

Jameson at high school swim meet, 2000

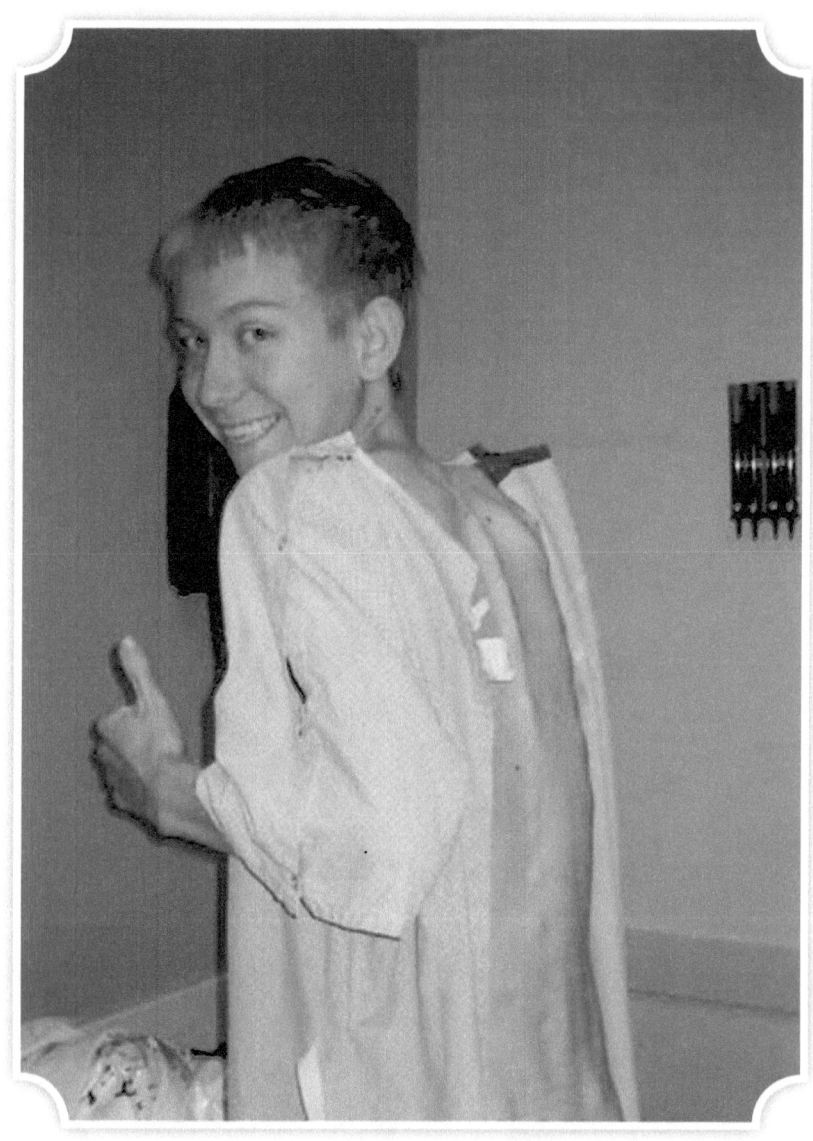

Jameson beginning his climb back

Jameson and Ivy

Ross on graduation day, May 2005

Jameson & Leah swimming with dolphins, May 2, 2006

Ross visiting Mexico City, 2006

Ross & Leah at Disneyland, April 2007

Jameson on graduation day from UGA, May 2007

Ross & Jameson in Tijuana, Mexico, 2008

Ross with new bass guitar on 21st birthday

Ross and His Princess Dory

Jameson skydiving, May 2009

The Atkinsons, 2019

Jameson & Ross, Christmas 2010

PART IV

THE OTHER SHOE DROPS

CHAPTER 24

December 2001

It had been a very emotionally-charged, exhausting seven months. The events of the past summer had definitely taken their toll on everyone. Although we realized that Jameson's sudden illness and subsequent lengthy recovery had greatly impacted our entire family, Steve and I really didn't think Ross had incurred any major long lasting disturbance in his life. We had done our best to make certain that his world had remained as normal as possible. He continued to have friends over regularly, and we were always transporting him to various social gatherings.

But one harrowing night completely changed our thinking.

We had noticed a few subtle changes in Ross for a couple of months; we attributed them to being a freshman in high school and to having normal teenage male hormone dysfunction. He had become moody, more argumentative, and would at times become angry at, what we considered, trivial situations. A prime example of this behavior had occurred Christmas Eve.

Ross had been wanting an electric guitar, so that was to be his main Christmas gift. As was our Atkinson family tradition, we allowed the opening of one or two gifts on Christmas Eve (the number depended on the total amount of gifts). We thought it would be humorous for Ross to open a toy guitar on Christmas Eve. We thought wrong!

Upon opening this grand gift, his mood immediately went sour. Things rapidly seemed to go from bad to worse. Ross became more and more agitated, even after the realization that the guitar was a practical joke. The more agitated Ross became, the angrier Steve was.

Finally, a yelling match ensued (this unfortunately became a standard of living in our home). It took my own yelling, that of the berserk family matriarch, to diffuse the situation. I had let loose with some sort of guilt-trip tirade about "ruining Christmas and I wasn't going to let that happen and I was sick of them arguing." I'm sure I also threw in some crocodile tears.

Whatever threats, pleas, and ultimatums that I had bellowed out seemed to have diffused the situation almost as quickly as it had ignited. We ended up having a very nice, pleasant, quiet Christmas. All had appeared to be going well over the next several days. Then we got the phone call.

The sudden ringing of the phone woke me from a deep sleep. It was 1:27 a.m. Steve and I had naturally been asleep for quite a while. Since it was Christmas break from school, Ross had been staying up long after the two of us called it a night.

On the telephone line was a young male voice, addressing me by name. When I answered the phone, I had assumed it would turn out to be a wrong number. Upon hearing my name, I presumed my assumption was incorrect. The caller explained that he was a friend of Ross's.

The young man proceeded to tell me that I needed to go check on Ross. He went on to explain that he was online on the computer with Ross as we spoke, and that Ross had admitted to taking a large dose of a cold medication. The friend thought we should know so we could make certain that Ross was okay. He also asked that I not tell Ross who the snitch was. I assured him that we wouldn't mention his name, and I sincerely thanked him for calling us.

After hanging up, I was in a total state of disbelief. Why would Ross do something like that? By this time, Steve was fully awake and had heard my end of the conversation, disjointed as it had been. I told him what Ross's friend had relayed to me.

I felt like the proverbial deer in the headlights- what should we do? After hearing my explanation of the entire conversation, Steve immediately said we had to go check on Ross and make sure he *was* alright. I automatically got out of bed and followed him. It was like a reflex action, because I certainly had not wanted to go and confront the situation. It wasn't that I didn't care; I was very concerned about Ross, but hadn't I been confronting situations non-stop since May! Couldn't I just have stayed curled-up in my bed and not been forced to handle reality?

We found Ross sitting at the computer; he looked fine, like nothing out of the ordinary was happening. Steve and I had agreed upon a little white lie. We wouldn't tell Ross about the phone call, mainly to protect his friend.

Our story went like this: The phone had awakened us (if questioned, we would say it had been a wrong number). We saw that Ross's bedroom light was still on, so we decided to find him and see why he was up so late.

After we had recited our speech, Steve casually mentioned to Ross that his eyes looked a little odd. He then moved toward Ross to get a closer look. He asked Ross if he had taken any kind of medicine; Ross said no. Steve pursued the issue, again mentioning to Ross that he didn't look quite right.

This time, Ross flatly replied that he had taken some type of medicine that he had found in the cabinet, but he didn't know what kind it was. After some investigative questioning, and also by taking inventory of the medications that we had on hand, I determined he hadn't taken anything lethal or that required his stomach to be pumped.

We of course wanted to know why he had taken medication. Ross replied that he wanted to see how it would make him feel, if it would make him feel better. He told us life was boring, and he needed to feel differently.

We stayed up talking with him for a while, trying to gain more insight into what was going on inside that head of his. Or maybe we were attempting to convince Ross, as well as ourselves, that everything would be alright.

After a time, the medication took its effect. Ross fell asleep and slept peacefully throughout the night. Upon returning to bed, Steve and I laid in the dark and talked. After Steve drifted back off to sleep, I continued to lie awake and worry. And think. I thought of being abruptly awakened by Jameson in the early morning hours of May 2.

I prayed that this outcome would be less traumatic.

CHAPTER 25

December 2002

Two thousand two had been a relatively uneventful year in the life of Ross. He and Jameson continued to simply tolerate each other. They both basically just tried to stay out of each other's way. Jameson believed that everything Ross did was stupid, and Ross showed no empathy for Jameson at all. There was, however, one unexpected incident.

Towards the end of 2001, Jameson had been interviewed by the city newspaper for an article detailing his illness and recovery. The piece was well-written and informative, and it also contained a candid photo of Jameson. I hung a copy of it in my laundry room, kind of as a momento. A short time later, while talking with Ross, the article was mentioned. To my astonishment, he began reciting its opening paragraph verbatim. Pretty impressive for someone who didn't want anything to do with his brother.

Since Ross had achieved sophomore status in high school, he was happy to no longer be considered an immature little freshman. The high point of his year had been the trip to Europe as a People to People Student Ambassador. Due to Jameson's illness the prior summer, causing Steve and I to be unwilling to let go of our baby boy for three weeks in a foreign land, we rescheduled Ross's journey for June of 2002.

He had not been very agreeable concerning the trip postponement when it occurred, but he wasn't really given much of a choice.

I must say, I was actually impressed with how he handled the entire trip. In order to tour the four countries that he was originally to visit—England, France, Italy and Greece—he had to travel with a group of kids from Michigan. Prior to these trips, the students would meet together, along with the chaperones, for several weeks in order to become acquainted with each other. When you live in Georgia, it's a little difficult to travel to Michigan on a regular basis for meet and greet sessions.

In order for Ross to at least meet some of his fellow travelers, Steve took him to Detroit for one of the meetings. While there, they also visited some museums and spent time with Steve's uncle. They both agreed they had a nice weekend together.

When the departure date for the trip arrived, Ross was ready to go. He didn't worry about not really knowing anyone. He assured me he would make friends and have a good time. He was able to call us a few times while he was away, and he genuinely sounded like he was having fun. He seemed to particularly enjoy Greece and Italy and told me that I really should go visit them one day. At the end of the trip, the chaperones were extremely complimentary of my son. And, from the report that I received from them, Ross did exactly what he had promised.

He had also formed a band with Stephen and Travis, two of his best friends; they went by the name of Rusted Spoon. Since Ross was the drummer, all of their practices were naturally held at our house. It could be quite noisy, but I actually enjoyed having them there. At times their practices would turn into jam sessions, with more friends joining in on the fun. Having a band of his own had pretty much made him a happy camper, most of the time.

There were still the mood swings, the occasional disagreements with me, and the more frequent arguments with Steve. At times, it appeared as though the two of them tried to see who could actually be the more stubborn.

One such battle of witlessness occurred the day after Rusted Spoon played their first official concert. It had been held in our garage on a Saturday night. There had been a respectable turn-out, although Ross had become upset during the concert because people began wandering around, goofing off, instead of giving the band their undivided attention. The rock scene was a difficult one.

The aforementioned battle had taken place midday on Sunday. I had attended Sunday morning church service. Steve had opted to stay home, and I had decided to let Ross sleep in. I arrived home to the two of them in the garage, yelling and acting like a couple of banshees (now, I had never actually met a banshee, but their tirades were legendary).

From what I could piece together, Steve had decided that Ross had been sleeping long enough and had awakened him (Ross not being allowed to awaken on his own was always unpleasant). Ross's drum set was, of course, still in the garage from the previous night, and Steve wanted it back in the house. Ross had gotten angry, had evidently rudely voiced his grievances, and had royally ticked his father off.

When I arrived on the scene, Steve had already broken one of the drums by throwing it down a hill into our backyard, and Ross was in maniac mode. There was no calming him down or reasoning with him. He stormed into the house. I knew he needed time to calm down, so I remained outside with Steve, attempting to diffuse *him*.

After a few minutes, Ross emerged from the house. Now, a fact that must be pointed out—when Ross had entered the house, he had beautiful thick, brown, wavy hair that reached almost to the bottom of his neck. Upon emerging from the house, he had horrible thick, brown, straight hair that was unevenly short and misshapen. All that I could do was gasp, and then I began to cry. I hadn't realized how nice his hair was, until he had ruined it.

When asked what he had done, Ross coolly replied that he had cut his hair (well, it didn't take a rocket scientist to figure that out!). When asked why he had done it, he had simply replied, "Because I could." Wow! He had sure taught us a lesson, and showed us who was boss!

As frustrating as the entire incident was, it had brought Steve and me both to the realization that Ross felt as though he didn't have control over a lot of things. We weren't certain if his age played a large factor in those feelings, or if it pertained more to the added attention that his brother had required for the past year and a half. A psychologist friend had commented a few months earlier that Ross simply could not compete with Jameson, so he attracted attention in his own way. She added that neither of them was to blame, that was simply the way it was. Ross also displayed more signs of frustration and anger than his friends. Either way, what he did have control over, we'd better watch out and be prepared for whatever he threw our way.

After everyone had calmed down, and I had fished Ross's beautiful brown locks out the bathroom sink and placed them in a zip lock bag, we took pictures of Ross and his self-appointed hairstyle. I then took him to Hair Cuttery to have a proper haircut. I kept the zip lock bag of hair in my hope chest for years, until one day my son talked me into throwing it away.

It had become a good reminder of a bad situation.

Whereas Ross had encountered a relatively uneventful year, Jameson's year had been jam -packed. Aside from continued frequent IV line infections, his health had greatly improved. His weight and his stamina were both back to normal, his appetite was voracious, and he prepared and administered his own TPN each night. He had also been able to regain his confidence. He unabashedly relayed his story to friends and strangers alike. And, he enjoyed showing off his "battle scars".

For Jameson, the year's highlight had been his acceptance into Eckerd College, which was a good thing considering he had refused to apply to any other schools. Steve and I had been very excited and bursting with pride when he graduated, with honors, from high school, but we were overjoyed when he was both accepted into Eckerd and granted a partial scholarship. Although we had concerns about Jameson going so far away to college, I was actually rather excited. Yes, I would worry about him getting sick, or becoming dehydrated, or not eating properly. And I would definitely miss him. But I knew how badly he wanted this, and I was anxious for him to be able to prove himself.

Before he moved off to Florida, he received an invitation to spend three weeks at the University of Nebraska Medical Center located in

Omaha. He would be participating in their intestinal rehab program. One of the primary goals was to help people dependent on TPN be able to reduce their IV intake, which would hopefully lead to the eventual discontinuation of the TPN altogether. The program emphasized a healthy diet and necessary lifestyle changes.

Jameson was reluctant to attend the program. He didn't want to be away from his friends, and especially his girlfriend, for three weeks with his college departure date looming so close. I was also a bit skeptical about the program, but Steve and I both felt Jameson couldn't risk passing up the opportunity to at least try to decrease his TPN dependency.

Since each participant in the program was required to bring a partner, I got to tag along to Omaha. We all met Ross at the Atlanta airport upon his return from Europe. He arrived tired but excited to tell us about his trip. He also arrived with a suitcase full of souvenirs and dirty clothes (at least the dirty clothes wouldn't be my problem). Jameson and I boarded a plane four hours later for our adventure. We didn't anticipate how mundane our adventure would be.

Initially, we were told Jameson wouldn't be allowed to leave the hospital grounds during the entire three weeks. When that tidbit of information caused him to refuse to go, Steve made several phone calls to the program director in order to convince him to allow weekend passes. After much debate, the rule was changed. Steve and Ross even managed to come for a visit on our second weekend there. It was nice for the four of us to do some sightseeing. We visited the zoo, took advantage of eating out, and took in a movie. Having some freedom on the weekends helped, but the days still dragged by.

We were also told there would be other teenagers participating in the program. Jameson had looked forward to meeting others with similar health issues, especially people his own age. We had so far been unable to meet, or even speak with, anyone else diagnosed with short bowel syndrome. Upon arrival, we discovered the only other participant was a woman in her fifties, accompanied by her daughter. Jameson and I were both very disappointed. Fortunately, Lana and her daughter were fun to be around.

The days were fairly routine. Our mornings were usually filled with lab work, weigh-ins, educational classes, and eating. Some of the afternoons involved cooking classes; others were free time. We had a lot of free time. Jameson became so bored that I was even able to convince him to accompany me to the gym on several occasions.

During our stay, Jameson had a voracious appetite. We became quite well-known in the little grocery/snack shop. As a result of the large amount of food he was ingesting and all of the inactivity that went along with it, Jameson was actually able to decrease his TPN intake while at the same time gaining weight. By the time we headed home, he was only infusing TPN three nights a week. The program director had also recommended that Jameson contact an organization named The Oley Foundation that dealt with people on TPN. He wrote the information down, but decided not to contact them.

Upon his return, Jameson only had two and a half weeks before he had to be at college. The days were filled with gathering everything that was needed for his move to Florida. Most of his spare time was spent with his girlfriend.

Jameson had also learned the name of his future roommate, along with his contact information. He was a little concerned about how the boy would react concerning his health issues, not to mention the fact that his medical supplies would take up a bit of space in an already undersized dorm room. Jameson had decided to call the roommate and fill him in. He was very relieved to hear that his soon to be new friend had no issues whatsoever with any of the information that was thrown his way. They both were looking forward to getting acquainted and each beginning their college careers.

On the day of the big move, Jameson was very excited. Although it was difficult for him to leave his girlfriend, he was anxious to begin a new chapter in his life. Since new student orientation and parent orientation took place simultaneously, the three of us drove down in separate cars. Both cars were filled with all the essentials for successful dorm life.

Since the TPN bags took up so much refrigerator space, added to the fact that Jameson ate enough for a small army, he had obtained special permission to have an oversized mini refrigerator in his dorm room. Also, because of his medical needs, he had been offered the use of a large handicapped suite. He would've had the room all to himself, plus a private bathroom. He wouldn't even consider the offer. He wanted the normal college experience, so that's what he got—tiny old room, friendly but unique roommate, and public bathroom down the hallway.

It was an extremely hectic orientation. Besides all of the planned college activities, we met with the campus nurse to discuss Jameson's issues and to make certain she was comfortable caring for him. There ended up being two different nurses that filled the role throughout his freshman year, and they were both excellent. They made certain his health stayed on track, and would even phone me to provide updates. He also worked with a nutritionist, located in Boston, who was wonderful to work with.

Maria made him tow the line and take proper care of himself.

College orientation week also turned into new doctor week. Jameson had an initial visit with a gastrointestinal doctor who would be overseeing his care while he lived in Florida. This physician would also be responsible for writing his TPN orders. Another new friend was an oral surgeon. It had been discovered that Jameson required some minor gum surgery. The periodontist in Athens felt it best for him to have the procedure done in Florida so the healing process could be better monitored.

Everything had gone well, up until the night before classes began. I had stayed behind a few days after Steve left in order to be with Jameson for his dental procedure. I had a midmorning flight back home on the first day of classes. Jameson had offered to drive me to the airport, but I thought it would be better to ride the airport shuttle. Good call.

Our last evening together was very relaxing. We went out to dinner, and then spent the next couple of hours watching our favorite TV shows. Then, when it was time for him to leave my hotel room and head back to his dorm, Jameson had a near panic attack. He began saying he thought he had made a mistake moving to Florida, and he didn't know if he was ready or able to take care of himself all on his own.

I really hadn't expected that reaction. I knew there would be some tears between us, but I wasn't prepared for the true lack of faith in himself that he was exhibiting. On the outside, I tried to be comforting but firm. On the inside, I, too, was crumbling. I realized how difficult college was going to be for him. Freshman year is always hard; it's a whole new world to adjust to. To a person with severe medical disabilities, it can seem like an insurmountable challenge.

I felt terrible for Jameson, but I also knew, without a doubt, that he was up for the challenge. I am fully aware that some people strongly disagreed with Steve's and my decision not to interfere with Jameson's move to Florida. I'm sure our parenting skills were questioned, but we agreed it was Jameson's life, and we wanted him to lead as normal a life as possible. I did not even consider offering him to travel back home with me.

I listened while he voiced his fears and concerns, then he listened while I voiced reassurances and my pride for him. He gradually began to calm down, and I could sense the confidence and excitement once again taking over. As he was leaving that night, we hugged each other tightly and reiterated our love. We agreed not to see each other before I left the following day.

As he walked out the door, I reminded him, "You can do this, Jameson."

He flashed that smile of his and replied, "I know I can."

I left for home the next morning feeling proud, and at peace.

CHAPTER 26

May 2003

Life had continued to plod along. For the past five years I had been working at a long-term care facility by the name of Family Life Enrichment Center, FLEC, as its employees so fondly referred to it. I had concluded years before that my calling as a nurse was in the field of geriatrics; therefore, I was quite contented with my job, the majority of the time.

Steve was in his element at work, having risen to the position of plant manager at one of Johnson & Johnson's more profitable plants. He had always kidded that if he couldn't be the boss at home, he was happy to be the boss somewhere. And, it was my belief that having a teenage son at home made being at work that much more enjoyable.

Ah, speaking of Ross. He had become somewhat of a youthful Jekyll and Hyde—we were never quite sure which personality would be joining us at the dinner table. If you've ever heard of teen angst, we definitely were beginning to experience its existence. Don't get me wrong, Dr. Jekyll continued to grace us with his presence. Ross could still be rather enjoyable and, dare I say, even entertaining. When Steve would be out of town on business, Ross and I made it a tradition to eat out. And I truly enjoyed his company. He would amaze me with all of his tidbits of information involving various punk rock, hard rock, and classic rock bands. Any information you wanted to know, he usually could provide. He also delighted in quizzing me when songs would be played on the radio—what's the name of the song, who sang it, etc.

Then, there were those times when Mr. Hyde paid an unwelcome visit. The norm was that Ross and I got along pretty well, but there was usually friction between him and Steve. At times there was friction between everyone. Ross was not what I would consider violent, but he could have a temper. And there never was much warning preceding an outburst. 2003 had produced, among other things, a busted acoustic guitar, a hole in my dining room wall (my children were obviously attracted to punching walls), a tendency in Ross to run away on foot when angry, and a nasty attitude (not mine).

This latest hole in the wall was, in a way, a result of Ross's better judgment. While Jameson was home from college one weekend, the two had gotten into a tiff, nothing major. Well, Ross had become so angry at Jameson that he wanted to hit him. To avoid doing that, he punched the nearest thing available, which happened to be the dining room wall.

Despite all of his aforementioned teen angst, Ross was, for the most part, still just a kid at heart. He and Jameson had both been huge pro wrestling fans when they were younger; so much that they, along with their neighborhood friends, had built a wrestling ring in our basement when we lived in Pennsylvania. Who knows, their wrestling club could have been the model and inspiration for the 1999 movie *Fight Club* (most unlikely, since the movie was based on a book).

Although it had been a crude wrestling ring, made mostly from couch cushions strategically placed on the floor and rope tied from support pole to pole to mark the boundaries, it apparently had also been a beloved wrestling ring. Our house was the place to be during weekday afternoons after school. There would be a steady stream of boys entering through our front door, parading through our foyer and down our basement stairs, all for the fame and glory of being that day's victor, wrestling champ of Yardley Run. Okay, so it was more realistic to say that we had a large group of boys, all ages, sizes, personalities, and ethnic backgrounds, all converging on our house for some camaraderie and after-school fun.

Boy, were Steve and I stupid! Didn't we ever stop to think what would happen if one of those innocent children ever broke a bone or, better yet, received a concussion or something even worse? Thank heavens the Lord watches over fools, and praise be to God that nobody ever got hurt (bumps and bruises didn't count). We could have been sued, for all we were worth and then some, had someone actually gotten injured!

Well, suffice it to say, I must've been a very slow learner. It was drawing close to the end of Ross's sophomore year in high school. Steve had been asked to move back to Pennsylvania to oversee a project for Johnson & Johnson. I was devastated. I had grown quite accustomed to living back in the South. I had even tried to convince Steve that Ross and I could stay in Georgia while he moved back to Pennsylvania. Ross wasn't much help with this argument; he was excited about moving back to his former stomping grounds. But as excited as he was, he had also begun to realize that he would indeed miss his friends in Georgia.

Ross had a friend, Nigel, who was a bigger wrestling geek than Ross or Jameson could ever have aspired to be. Nigel was planning a big wrestling event to mark the end of the school year, but he didn't know where he was going to hold the event. He needed a big area, somewhere convenient to get to—enter our backyard and Ross's eagerness to be a part of this event. We lived on a corner lot with a very open backyard, and our neighborhood was very well-known and centrally located.

When Ross had broached me with the idea of holding this wrestling event in our yard, I had halfheartedly listened to his request and to the best of my recollection probably mumbled,

"We'll see." Of course, Ross took my response as a "most definitely-fine idea," and proceeded to inform Nigel that everything was a go.

When Ross reminded me about the Event a week before it was to take place, I was nearly speechless. I, in my naivety, had assumed the Event had been relegated to happen elsewhere, since Ross and I never discussed it again. I had never even mentioned anything about it to Steve, because I knew he would blow a gasket! Had I gotten myself into a pickle! And, the best part yet, the Event was going to be held on a Friday evening, Mother's Day weekend. The crew wanted to bring everything on Thursday afternoon and setup. I was having outpatient surgery on Thursday and Steve would be taking the day off. I couldn't even plan on everything being delivered while Steve was at work. I decided to do the only thing I thought I could do—I kept my mouth shut until the very last minute.

Thursday rolled around. Ross went to school as usual. Steve accompanied me to my outpatient surgery, which went off without a hitch. We got home from surgery early afternoon, and I decided to lie on the sofa for a while since I was still a little groggy and a little sore. I kept telling myself to stay calm and not to say anything until the last possible moment.

Well, that moment came when Ross arrived home from school all excited about the upcoming event. I tried to act nonchalant and to casually mention to Steve what was about to transpire. I told myself that I had just had surgery; surely, Steve would go a little easy on me.

Oh, he was not a happy man! Things became worse when all of the parts for the wrestling ring were being delivered. My, oh my, that was some wrestling ring! Not at all like the little one previously in our basement. There were an infinite number of large tires that continued to be rolled down the hill into our backyard. These tires were meticulously placed in order to form the foundation of the ring, the part that would give it its bounce.

Sheets of plywood were then placed on top of the tires to form the basis of the wrestling mat. Next came thick, flexible mats to complete the main portion of the ring. In each corner stood a thick pipe, welded into a tire rim for stability. From these four pipes was strung thick, elastic roping. This roping was used to designate the boundaries of the wrestling ring, just as in pro wrestling. Upon completion, it was a pretty impressive sight.

Now, we were originally supposed to drive to Steve's mother's house on Saturday before Mother's Day, but Steve was so upset about the whole wrestling fiasco that he decided to drive over on Friday after work—leaving me with the entire event on my shoulders! I guess I deserved it, and I'd really like to say I'd learned my lesson, but I probably hadn't.

The evening of wrestling was a huge success; a large crowd attended and the wrestlers put on a good show. There were probably fifteen to twenty cars parked on the street in front of our house. Also, the adult promoters of the event brought in ice chests full of sodas and various candies and other snack foods to be sold as refreshments. It was quite well-organized.

I ventured outside a couple of times to attempt to videotape some of the action; Ross sent me back inside each time. I did manage to obtain somewhat decent footage by standing at the kitchen window to film. Ross, who wrestled as his alter ego, Hardcore Ross Atkinson, enjoyed being in the limelight for a few minutes. Money was spent, refreshments were eaten, and most importantly, nobody was injured.

So, once again, my stupidity had not gotten me into any serious trouble—no lawsuits, no unruly mobs, no irreparable damage to our property. Our entire family came out of the whole situation pretty much unscathed. We even learned in later years to laugh about the Event.

I wish the same were true for every situation.

CHAPTER 27

August 2003

Our move back to Pennsylvania became a reality. All things considered, it had gone smoothly. At the time of our move, the housing market was pretty tight. Therefore, we didn't have a lot of houses to choose from. The available ones ran the gambit from too small, too old, bad location, too dated, too much traffic, and even too white (referring to the color of the siding, paint, carpet, and kitchen appliances). We finally settled on a large home in an upper middle class neighborhood. It was located in the same school district where we had formerly lived. For Steve, the house was love at first sight. For Ross, it seemed okay. For me, it was too much house, but I was pretty much outnumbered.

The summer leading up to our move was chaotic and stressful. Jameson had had a successful freshman year in college. His grades were good, he earned a certification in scuba diving, he made good friends, and his health remained stable. Yeah, he had some ups and downs with his weight and infections, and he even had a bout with an uncommonly large kidney stone, but overall he took remarkably good care of himself.

Despite all of that, Jameson decided a career in marine biology wasn't for him, so he decided to transfer to a college in Georgia. Ironically, he moved back to Georgia as the rest of us prepared to move back to

Pennsylvania. Steve and I tried to convince him to move with us, but he was definitely against the idea. He loved living in Athens, and he didn't want to leave his girlfriend again.

A couple of weeks after he returned home from Florida, he ended up in the hospital with a severe case of pancreatitis. He made a full recovery, but that episode started me on the path of really dreading to move. I treated Steve horribly (again). I knew he really didn't have much choice in the matter, but I placed the blame on him anyway. I was miserable, so I certainly wanted him to be miserable also. I cried. I yelled. I tried to bargain. I even stormed out of the house and ran away (I drove to a friend's house and hid my van so Steve couldn't find me).

Nothing worked. I was doomed to move back to Pennsylvania and desert my ill son. I knew he couldn't possibly make it on his own, a second time, without my ever present guidance. As skeptical as I was of prayer at that point, I asked God continually to make it so we wouldn't have to move.

Then one night, God literally answered me. Steve was out of town; both boys were out for the evening, so I was home alone. I was lying in bed, attempting to relax and read before I went to sleep. I simply couldn't concentrate on what I was reading. I felt the urge to pray, so I began to do just that; it was actually begging and pleading more so than praying.

I was fervently asking God to please allow me to remain in Athens. I explained that I couldn't bear the thought of moving so far away and leaving Jameson all on his own. I snorted and cried and proceeded to remind God that He had allowed Jameson to become ill, so now didn't He owe it to me to do something to prevent our move?

That's when it happened. I really can't put it into words, but I know God spoke to me. It was as if I could actually hear Him speaking, like He was standing at the foot of my bed.

"I want you to move. Jameson will be fine."

I was awestruck. All I could say was, "Okay, Lord. I'll move."

After our little talk, I felt at peace concerning the move. I still didn't want to go, but the crushing weight I carried around felt as though it had been lifted off of me.

Since we were selling our house, we purchased a condo for Jameson to live in. Because he would be living in his own place, I don't think he minded our move at all. Of course, there had to be a touch of drama thrown in. Jameson's move in date kept being pushed farther and farther back, to the point where he moved in only a few days before we moved out. In fact, our realtor, along with the maintenance crew at the condominium complex, actually volunteered to move Jameson's furniture and belongings in for him.

Just when I felt that everything might turn out alright, Ross had thrown me a curve. It was the night before the movers came. Ross's friends had given him a going away party. When he arrived home, he said he had a good time, but he acted subdued. Not normal post-party attitude for Ross. I felt he was probably a little sad about moving, but Ross wasn't one to show his emotions very easily.

After a few minutes of the three of us chatting, Steve and I went on to bed; the next day would be tiring. Ross decided to watch TV in the basement for a while, one last time. After going to bed, I simply could not go to sleep, so I decided to visit with Ross for a bit. When I didn't find him in the basement, I stepped out onto the lower patio to see if he was outside. There he was, squatting down behind one of the rocking chairs, smoking a cigarette.

The sight of him smoking caught me off guard, but what really shook me was how alone he looked. He didn't look like a fifteen year old teenager—he looked like a scared little boy. Though I was disappointed that he was smoking, I couldn't be mad at him. I felt overwhelming sorrow for him. When I asked him what he was doing, he blundered something about "trying to calm down because he was leaving all of his friends."

My heart ached for him, but I knew there was nothing I could say that would make him feel better. I walked over and kissed him on the top of his head, told him I was sorry, and asked him not to stay up too late. As I left him, alone in the dark, and made my way back to my bedroom, I cried—for innocence lost, and for things unknown.

CHAPTER 28

February 2004

The move back to Pennsylvania had gone smoothly, but the transition had not. The grass on the other side was not quite as green as Ross had anticipated. Colin, one of Ross's best friends from childhood, threw him a surprise sixteenth birthday party only a few weeks after our move. He also made numerous other attempts to help Ross settle back into life in Pennsylvania, but too many changes had taken place over the years. Kids grow up and choose different paths, and old friendships become strained. Different personalities, different tastes in music and entertainment, different coping methods come to light.

So was life for Ross. Punk rock had become a big part of his music scene and also his lifestyle. In the months following our move, he had made a new group of friends. Some of them were endearing, others were not. Ross and Steve also had begun to have frequent arguments and fights. When the two of them would argue, it would at times cause me to react irrationally. During one such argument, I had become so upset with Steve that I demanded he leave. When he refused, I called 911 in order to have a policeman come and remove him. That move really didn't help the situation! Steve finally agreed to go, and then I had to convince the officer that his assistance wasn't necessary.

Steve reluctantly spent the night at a motel, and I worried that I had caused irreparable damage to our marriage. Thankfully, I hadn't; we were able to work through our differences. We basically agreed to disagree. We had learned over the years that our marriage was strong enough to survive life's challenges.

Ross also had begun to have days when he would literally refuse to get up and go to school, no matter what threats were made or punishments were handed out. My son had become very angry and defiant. There had also been numerous times when Ross would become mad at me or Steve and simply run away from the house on foot. Luckily, he would always come back after a while. One positive aspect of Ross's new life was his part time job. He wasn't particularly fond of it, but it did occupy quite a bit of his spare time.

Things had really begun to escalate by February. And, I really never decided if this was a blessing or a curse, but Steve had been transferred back to Georgia after only six months. I had decided it would probably be better if Ross and I stayed put until the school year was over in June. Steve came back sporadically for short visits. It was just Ross and me in the big, rambling house.

I was having some issues of my own. Since our move back, all my former friends had either moved away or were working full-time. In my semi-depressed state, I felt as though I had to have something to occupy my time. I had begun taking a medical refresher course for nurses. The class met one evening a week from 6:00 until 10:00 p.m.

I knew Ross had become a cigarette smoker, but since moving back to Pennsylvania, Steve and I had both begun to suspect that he was also smoking marijuana. One day, while Ross was at school, I decided to do what any concerned and loving parent would do—I snooped. I turned into Detective Mom in order to find evidence to either support our theory, or hopefully, dispel it.

Now, my son could be quite devious, but apparently not real intelligent at times. After asking myself where a teenager would hide his pot, I discovered it in the first place I looked, a shoe box in the top of Ross's bedroom closet. My heart sank! I had never seen marijuana before, but I instinctively knew that is what I had discovered. Part of me thought, "Couldn't you have hidden it better than this?" What would be my next step now that I had?"

Besides having to attend my nursing class that evening, Steve was flying in from Georgia later that night for a long weekend. He was supposed to arrive at the Philadelphia airport around 10:30 p.m., so I was going to leave straight from class and go pick him up. I really didn't want to get into a big argument with Ross concerning the pot before I went to class. I felt I needed ample time to discuss the situation with him. On the other hand, I couldn't bear the thought of leaving the marijuana where I found it—I felt that would be condoning its use. I decided to flush the pot down the toilet and leave the empty bag in the shoe box, hoping Ross would think he had already smoked all of it and had just forgotten. Then when the time was right we could all sit down and have a civil discussion.

The afternoon was rather routine after Ross got home from school. We had an early dinner, I reminded him that I was picking Steve up from the airport straight after class, and then I went to class.

Thankfully, Steve's flight was on time. As we were driving home from the airport, Ross called to ask what time we would be arriving home. We told him around 11:30 p.m. He replied okay; he had just been wondering.

I had driven my minivan to the airport. Steve's old Nissan Maxima, which we had kept as an extra car, always stayed parked in front of the garage. As we pulled into the driveway, Steve commented, "Oh, you parked the Maxima in the garage." To which I replied, "No I didn't."

He looked over at me and said, "Well, it's not here." It was at that moment that I realized, no indeed, the Maxima was not parked in its usual place. Ross must have taken the car somewhere.

The kicker was—Ross didn't have a driver's license.

As soon as we got into the house and made certain that Ross was not home, I called him on his cell phone to find out where he was. We had actually kind of hoped that the car had been stolen; that would have been easier to deal with than whatever was in store for us concerning Ross's joy ride! Ross explained that he was on his way home from Philly and that he would be home shortly.

Steve and I were both livid. We couldn't believe Ross had taken the car without permission, and then had driven all the way into Philadelphia, with no driver's license. He had never even driven on an interstate before! What had he been thinking?

As it turned out, he had been doing a lot of thinking, but not very mature thinking. Ross arrived home around 12:15 a.m., acting very stoically and very matter- of-factly. Upon calmly questioning him, we got a good picture of the evening's events. Those events were as follows:

1. After I left for class, Ross went to get his stash of pot
2. Found the pot was gone, an empty bag in its place
3. Freaked out (loss of good pot plus the knowledge that I was apparently on to him)
4. Confirmed that he hated his life in Pennsylvania
5. Called and consulted with various friends
6. Decided to take drastic measures
7. Decision made to runaway to Georgia
8. Took car without permission and drove to Philadelphia airport
9. Parked car in long-term parking and rode shuttle to airport
10. Phoned another friend who informed him that he wouldn't be allowed to buy a ticket because he was underage
11. Distraught—took the shuttle back to long-term parking and retrieved car
12. Didn't know what else to do, so started drive home
13. Accidentally took wrong exit off interstate
14. Drove through Philly in the wrong direction home
15. Ended up in King of Prussia, Pennsylvania
16. Had no idea how to get home
17. Called girlfriend (who lived in Georgia) and explained dilemma
18. Girlfriend got on MapQuest and found directions from King of Prussia back to our house
19. She stayed on the phone with Ross, giving him directions, until he recognized where he was

20. Ross phoned Steve and me to see when we would arrive at home from the airport. He had hoped to beat us home so we wouldn't know he had taken the car and tried to leave Pennsylvania
21. The unexpected detour caused Ross to arrive home after we did
22. Life sucked for everyone involved
23. Thanked God for keeping Ross safe while on the road, and for keeping him out of jail

Steve and I fought to keep our composure throughout the conversation, and resisted the urge to have a yelling match. We were all tired and miserable. Ross was almost grounded for life, but not quite. He accepted his punishment without complaint.

Other times did not end as amicably.

CHAPTER 29

March 2004

We had been living back in Pennsylvania for approximately six and a half months, and life was getting worse. With Steve working and living back in Georgia, at least there was less conflict between him and Ross. Unfortunately, my relationship with Ross was crumbling. The two of us had always gotten along pretty well and had been able to resolve our conflicts relatively unscathed. But, to revamp a phrase from a Bob Dylan song, the times were a changing.

Ross had gradually become more sullen and defiant, and I didn't like him very much. My patience had worn very thin, and we managed to argue all the time. March seemed to be a particularly volatile month for some reason. I think the joy riding incident the previous month had really fueled the fire.

I knew for a fact that he, unfortunately, continued to use pot. I had again checked his hiding place, and there it was. After flushing it down the toilet, I decided to try an experiment. Instead of leaving the empty bag, I filled it with oregano (looks like pot but smells much better). Ross never mentioned anything concerning the little incident, but that ended the illegal use of at least the shoe box.

One afternoon after school, we had—once again—gotten into an argument. Looking back, I sometimes think we argued because we weren't sure what else to do. To further prove that theory, I couldn't even begin to tell you what we had been arguing about on that particular afternoon; it could have been anything from disagreeing on the color of the grass to deciding what to eat. I do know most of our arguments started off dumb and escalated to moronic.

After we had begun arguing, Ross went upstairs to his bedroom—his safe haven. He particularly liked his room because it had a large bonus room attached to it. We had finished out the bonus room shortly after we moved into the house in an attempt to help Ross adjust to the move (since he discovered it wasn't nearly as much fun as he had anticipated). The bonus room was somewhat akin to teen paradise—it housed drums, guitars, basses, amplifiers, a sixty-four-inch TV, lounging furniture, and various other teenage accessories. Plus, it was virtually soundproof; that was good for everyone involved.

Awhile after Ross had stormed up to his room, my cell phone rang. It was Ross, calling on his cell phone. He asked if I knew where he was. I replied that I assumed he was in his room. He made some type of snide remark and informed me that I was wrong. Of course, I took the bait and went upstairs. Ross was correct; he wasn't in his room, or the bonus room. I did notice one of the windows in the bonus room was wide open.

The little turd had climbed out of the window and was nowhere in sight! The first thought I had was, "Oh please, don't let any of the neighbors have seen him climbing out! They *will* think we are crazy!" Now I was fuming. How dare he sneak out on me!

We played phone tag for about an hour. I would call him and he would either both answer and then hang up on me, or he wouldn't answer at all. Then every so often he would call me to taunt me. I believe I probably hung up on him once or twice. I learned that he had taken his bicycle and ridden away, but I didn't know which direction he had gone, or where he was. I could just picture the police stumbling upon him and arresting him for some crazy reason.

Finally, he broke down and told me where he was; then he asked if I could come and pick him up. Of course, I did. I didn't want to take the chance of him changing his mind and really running away. I found him sitting on a curb in a neighborhood three or four miles away from our house. I silently loaded both him and his bicycle into the van. I don't think we talked a lot that night after returning home; we realized how idiotic both of us had acted earlier.

We also both learned that, no matter what the situation, if I could help Ross in some way, I would certainly try my very best to do so.

CHAPTER 30

March 2004

As I mentioned previously, March did seem to have been a very volatile month. The fights continued over Ross going to school in the mornings, as did fights and arguments in relation to most every other subject on the face of this earth. One argument in particular was very nasty, so much in fact it became downright violent.

It started out like any other argument. I really wish I could relate to you the facts and the subject matter, but for the life of me I can't remember what the argument was about, or how it began. All I remember is that it became very heated. We yelled and screamed and, I'm sure, said hurtful things to each other.

In a moment of desperation, I even phoned a psychologist that had tested Ross for ADD (attention deficit disorder) and asked for his advice. I explained to him that Ross had become very unruly and disrespectful to me, and I felt as though I couldn't handle him anymore. The psychologist recommended that I contact a teenage halfway house in the area and see if he could be admitted the next morning (it was too late in the day for same day admission).

When I related to Ross what the psychologist had told me, he really became agitated. He began yelling at me to do it, to call and see if he could be admitted. He said it would be a way for me to get rid of him.

He even went and packed an overnight bag. Then I began to crumble. I started to cry, and then I turned into a blathering idiot. I couldn't even think straight.

All of this made Ross even madder. He became uncontrollable. He began ranting and raving, and then he grabbed a dish off of the kitchen counter and threw it to the floor. A small ceramic bunny that he had given me as a birthday gift one year sat on a low dividing wall separating the kitchen from the family room. I loved that bunny. He picked the figurine up and held it in the air, as if it were some type of bargaining chip. I was crying and screaming and begging him to put the rabbit back down. He did all right; he smashed it into a million pieces on my kitchen floor.

As I was hyperventilating over my lost memento, Ross picked up a kitchen chair and threw it against the sliding glass doors. I let out a scream that probably could be heard in the next town. I'm not sure if the scream was more out of anger or more from disbelief that he had attempted to shatter the sliding glass doors. Fortunately, the kitchen chair wasn't that heavy, and the glass door was pretty durable.

I had had it! I also was afraid of what Ross might do next. Without really thinking, I grabbed my phone and dialed 911. Ross was yelling and going up the stairs to his room. I was thinking, "I'll show him!" When the dispatcher answered the call, I simply reported that my son had gotten out of control and was breaking things and that I didn't feel safe. The dispatcher asked if I felt as though I needed to get out of the house. I replied no, that things had calmed down somewhat. She acquired all of the necessary information and told me a police officer would arrive shortly. I thanked her and hung up. And then I thought, "What have I done?"

Actually, I was too mad to really care what I had done. I probably could've been described as livid. I grabbed a hammer and headed up the stairs. I wasn't sure if I took the hammer with me for protection, or for use as a weapon. When I arrived at Ross's room, he had locked himself in. I calmly went and got one of the skeleton keys used to unlock the interior doors, and I let myself in.

Ross was lying in bed. He told me to go away; he didn't want to talk to me. If there's one thing I'm known for, it's being persistent. If I am in a mood to talk or argue, I can usually wear down even the most stoic person. I had met my match in Ross. He just lay there, staring at me. The only thing he flatly muttered was, "You called the cops on me."

As I stood there tightly gripping the hammer, I suddenly had the urge to hit something. I use the pronoun something loosely, because honestly, I felt like hitting someone, but I knew I would immediately regret doing that. Plus, I didn't fancy going to jail. Then I had a brilliant idea; I could retaliate and take my anger out on something that Ross held in very high esteem, something that he loved.

"Okay!" I spat out. "I'll show you!"

I stormed into the bonus room, took my hammer, and wham!

I hit the screen of the big, beautiful, sixty-five-inch television as hard as I could. A small hole appeared with several rather long cracks radiating from it. Since the screen was made of a hard plastic, the TV would still be watchable, but somewhat distorted.

Proudly, I marched back into his bedroom. "I busted your TV," I announced.

Ross replied, "So? I think you're the crazy one. Maybe the police should haul you away."

About that time, the front doorbell rang.

"There they are," he said, "go tell them how crazy I am."

I suddenly felt nauseous. How was I going to handle this? I didn't want Ross arrested. I just wanted my former son back.

I opened the door and spoke with the officer. After a few moments, I finally convinced him that Ross had calmed down and that I no longer felt threatened. He told me not to hesitate to call back if I felt the need to. I assured him again that everything was under control, and I politely thanked him.

As the officer left and I closed the front door, I stood there hoping, once again, that none of the neighbors had witnessed the fiasco at my house. After a few moments, and a few deep breaths, I climbed the stairs once again to Ross's room. As I walked in, Ross asked, "So, are they going to arrest me?"

I told him no. I also told him that I had explained to the policeman that he had calmed down and that everything seemed to be alright. Ross then stated that he was tired and was going to sleep. That was fine with me; I didn't have any fight left in me. I told him good night and closed his door. I was emotionally and physically drained. I wondered what type of dilemma we would find ourselves in next.

I didn't have to wonder for very long.

CHAPTER 31

March 27, 2004

Steve had been very close to his mother's uncle and his wife all of his life. As a matter of fact, it was because of his Uncle Tom that Steve and I even met in the first place.

As a teenager, I attended church with Tom and Olline "Lene" Wood, and they had become close friends with my parents. Miss Olline was honestly the world's best cook, and Mr. Tom was one of the most sincere Christian men you could ever meet. Back in the fall of 1977, Mr. Tom required back surgery. I had gone to the hospital to visit him, and it just so happened that his extremely handsome, blue-eyed great-nephew was coming to visit on the same day. Naturally, I extended the length of my visit so that I might have the opportunity to meet nephew Steve. We began dating a few months later.

Steve and I both remained close to Uncle Tom and Aunt Lene throughout our marriage, and would have dinner with them whenever we were in town. Unfortunately, Aunt Lene had fallen and broken her hip in November, and never fully recovered. Sadly, she had slipped into a coma and wasn't expected to live much longer. Since Steve was living back in Georgia, he had already traveled to Macon to be at her bedside. I had arranged a flight out of Philly for Sunday morning, March 28.

Ross and I had been tolerating each other fairly well. We pretty much avoided the subject of the crazy mother and son/ bashed TV incident (for years thereafter my reputation as the crazed hammer-wielding mother was well-known among Ross's peers) . We enjoyed having dinner together at night. We would watch some of our favorite TV shows together. And we would sometimes go to the movies together. Ross was even getting home before his curfew on the weekends.

On this particular Saturday night he was hanging out with some friends at one of their houses. One of the friends was old enough to drive, so he was going to bring Ross home. Ross had agreed to be home by eleven o'clock since I wanted to see him before I left for Georgia, and I knew he wouldn't be up early on Sunday morning.

I had been lying in bed reading and was getting rather sleepy. The clock read ten fifteen. I decided to call Ross, just to make certain he was on schedule. He answered his phone after a few rings and proceeded to tell me that, "They were on their way to drop him off." I hung up and thought that I might actually get to go to sleep a little earlier than I had anticipated.

After I spoke with Ross, I apparently dozed off. I was jolted awake at ten forty-five by the telephone ringing. I thought it was probably Steve. Instead it was Ross. "You need to come pick me up."

"I thought they were bringing you home."

"You need to come pick me up at the police station."

Now mind you, that was a phrase I had subconsciously been expecting to hear for a while, but I was thrown completely off guard.

"The police station!" I exclaimed. "What are you doing at the police station?"

"Just come and get me," he demanded. "I'm at the Lower Makefield Township one—it's behind the township building. Hurry up!"

My mind was racing as I drove to get him. What on earth had he done? I had just spoken with him on the phone thirty minutes ago. Had he been caught stealing? Trying to buy beer? Oh my lord! Had he been caught with drugs? How was I going to handle this?

When I walked into the police station and told them my name and who I was there for, I was ushered through a door and into a hallway.

There were other parents already there; some I recognized and some I didn't. Like me, none of them looked very happy.

I was then introduced to a detective and ushered into a small conference room. There sat Ross, looking defiant and very much like a juvenile delinquent. The detective explained that because the boys were underage, they hadn't been arrested, but they were brought in for destroying private property. I felt myself draw in a breath. He went on to explain that they had been picked up for smashing mailboxes.

It just so happened that at some point in his young life, Ross had made a list of things he wanted to accomplish. Guess what was on that list? Yep! *Smash mailboxes with a baseball bat.* Strike that one off the list!

I could barely look at my son, and I dared not say anything to him. I was so frustrated! How could he have been so stupid!

The detective finished giving Ross a speech and explaining the next steps in the whole process. The boys didn't have a criminal record, but they certainly weren't going to get off too easily. Community service, going before a judge, apologizing to homeowners, paying for damages—it was a fun process. He scheduled Ross to come back in a week and a half so the punishment details could be finalized.

I sincerely thanked the detective and we left. As we walked out of the police station, Ross pointed to a police car and nonchalantly stated, "That's the one I was in. It was cool riding in the back of a police cruiser."

I just stared at him. As I shook my head, the only thing I could think of to say was, "Did they handcuff you?"

"No," he replied, "but that would have been awesome!"

On the ride home, I found out the details of the debaucherous evening. It seemed the boys had had a pretty boring evening. As they were preparing to leave their friend's house, Ross casually mentioned it would be fun to smash a mailbox; the others agreed. Of course, it had to be Ross who planted the seed. After rounding up a couple of baseball bats, the boys headed toward our house, taking out a few mailboxes along the way.

Here came the good part. Due to their jubilant mood, the driver got a little reckless with his driving; this was observed by a policeman on patrol. The police officer then pulled our renegade boys over, probably to give them a lecture. As the officer approached the driver to have a chat, he couldn't help but notice the passengers in the backseat attempting to stow an object into the trunk of the car by way of a partially folded-down backseat. As he explained to the driver the reason for being pulled over, he kept his eye on the three boys in the backseat.

After a few moments, the officer shone his light into the backseat. "I see you boys have got a baseball bat back there. You haven't been using that on any mailboxes, have you?"

It was never made quite clear who the respondent was, but from the darkened backseat there came a reply.

"Yes sir."

Now, we'd always taught both of our sons not to lie and to always tell the truth, but I must admit, I honestly hoped my son was not the one to "fess up." Yes, what they did was wrong, and yes, they deserved punishment for it, but sometimes it's just better to keep quiet. I am aware that line of thinking makes me a full blown hypocrite. Hey, I'm sorry, but I'm only human. I do always try to admit to my own faults.

You already basically know what happened after our happy little group was pulled over. Even though I was in dire need to vent to my husband and recount the evening's festivities to him, I realized there was no need to burden him at such a late hour. I thought it better just to wait and fill him in when I saw him in person in a few short hours. I threatened Ross that for the brief period of time I was away in Georgia, he was not to leave the house except to go to school. As a good faith measure, I took the extra set of car keys with me so as not to have a repeat of the infamous borrowed car episode. I also had a good friend to check up on him a few times.

I had hoped the run-in with the law would shake Ross up a bit and encourage him to make better decisions. I considered the incident to be a learning experience and thought it might pave the way for an attitude adjustment.

It did turn out to somewhat adjust Ross's attitude, but not in a positive way.

CHAPTER 32

March 31, 2004

It had been a long few days, and I was happy to be back home. My trip to Georgia had been timed just right. Aunt Olline had passed away while I was in flight to be with her. So although I wasn't at her bedside when she died, I was able to spend quality time with Steve, Uncle Tom, and my parents throughout the planning of the funeral arrangements and the funeral itself. Steve was somewhat aghast concerning Ross's escapade the previous night, though realistically, he wasn't overly surprised.

My flight home left a few hours after the funeral. Unfortunately, for various reasons, my plane was diverted to Washington D.C. and grounded for quite some time before again taking off for Philadelphia, where we were caught in a holding pattern forever. I finally arrived home between one thirty and two o'clock in the morning. I would have loved to have slept late that morning, but I needed to be up to make certain Ross was up and off to school. While I was out of town, he apparently went to school and stayed out of trouble.

It was mid to late morning, and I was cleaning the kitchen when my phone rang. I answered with a jovial hello, expecting it to be one of my friends calling. Instead, it was a woman who identified herself as the principal's secretary from the high school.

She asked if she was speaking to Mrs. Atkinson; I confirmed that she was.

The secretary went on to explain that Ross had been involved in a fight, which he instigated, during gym class. Neither he nor the other boy had been seriously injured; Ross was receiving three days of in-school suspension. We would then have to meet with the principal to determine whether he would be expelled from school or even allowed to return to school.

I was basically speechless throughout the conversation. I heard myself at one point ask, "Ross? In a fight?" I then asked who he had been in a fight with. The reply stunned me—it was one of his friends.

I hung up the phone in a state of confusion; what the heck just happened? Ross definitely had a temper and could sometimes lose it in an instant, but he avoided physical contact at all costs. A couple of years prior, he had punched a hole in my dining room wall in order to avoid hitting Jameson during an argument. Ross, in a fight? Especially with someone he considered a friend? It made absolutely no sense to me. As I stood there with my mind reeling, my phone rang again. Oh lord, what now?

It was a friend of mine calling to see how my trip was. I found it very difficult to concentrate on our conversation, considering the news I had just received. I was still trying to clear my head from all of the events that had taken place over the weekend. I didn't know how I was reasonably going to deal with this new problem. Now I really felt alone. Steve was my only confidant in matters of Ross, and he was eight hundred miles away in Georgia. Plus, he had plenty to worry about with his new job. And I really didn't feel as though I could fully open up to any of my friends concerning all of the problems I was dealing with. They all seemed to have perfect children—no anger issues, no drugs, no hostility, no defiance, no rebellion, no apathy towards school, and certainly no run- ins with the law. Oh, poor me! I felt as though life had already dealt me a hard enough blow with Jameson, now things were going to hell in a hand basket with Ross. Ah, the uncertainty of life.

I honestly can't say how I spent my day from the time I received the phone call from school until Ross arrived home, but I'm pretty sure anxious and sitting on pins and needles would both accurately have described my state of being. I was waiting at the door when Ross came in.

"What happened today?" I immediately asked.

"So you know about it," he responded.

"I know you were in a fight in gym class," I replied.

"It wasn't a fight. I punched him in the head," Ross stated matter-of-factly.

Apparently, Ross's friend Shaun had become less of a friend and more of a bully. According to Ross, Shaun had been taunting him and belittling him for some time, and he just couldn't take it anymore. So during gym class, when the taunting began again, Ross started punching Shaun in the head. The gym coach intervened; Shaun never offered to throw a punch to defend himself. He also refused to file any type of complaint against Ross.

Shaun was either the bigger person in that situation and showed more maturity, or he knew he had been at fault. I chose to believe the latter. Although Ross had caused me nothing but grief and pain over the past few months, I wanted to hold on to the belief that my son's better qualities still existed.

When I asked Ross why he hadn't mentioned that Shaun was causing him problems, he answered that he wasn't going to go crying to his mommy that somebody was being mean to him. I assumed I could count his response as a slight sign of maturity.

After discussing the day's events with Steve, we decided and agreed upon an immediate plan of action. We realized how unhappy Ross must have been, and we feared what might happen next. After all, if within five days' time he had managed to be hauled into the police station *and* threatened with the possibility of being expelled from school, what else did we have to look forward to?

Spring break was in one week; Ross and I had plans to go to Georgia for that week. The revamped plan was, I would return to Pennsylvania alone after spring break. Steve and I both spoke with school officials in Georgia and were able to expedite a transfer for Ross for the remainder of the school year. We were scared not to. And I honestly didn't think I could handle another two months of misery, for the both of us.

Before the transfer could occur, we had loose ends to tie up. First came our meeting with the school principal, after Ross had completed his in-school suspension. I was a nervous wreck, even though I knew Ross would be transferring from the school. Ross was his normal nonchalant self.

The principal explained that Ross was fortunate because the police weren't called in when the altercation occurred. He went on to say that a lot of times the police did become involved, and if Shaun's parents decided to press charges, we would be notified. I sat there thinking, "Well, at least the police already know Ross; how cozy."

Ross would be allowed to remain in school because he had no prior disciplinary problems on his record, but if he got into trouble again, he would be kicked out. My stomach was in knots, even though I knew Ross only had four more days to keep his nose clean and stay out of trouble.

After the principal had his say, I explained (stretched the truth) that we were being transferred back to Georgia, and that Ross would not be returning to Pennsbury High School after spring break (did the principal look a little relieved?). The principal wished him well and offered any assistance necessary to make the transition. As I left the school I reminded Ross to please stay out of trouble.

Whew, one meeting down, one to go!

Two days later, we were sitting in the conference room at the police station, meeting with the detective in charge of the mailbox-bashing case. I pleaded our case of moving out of the area and back to Georgia and asked what Ross needed to do in order to fulfill the necessary requirements for his probation, since he wouldn't be available for the community service or to keep his appointment with the judge.

The detective stated if we paid our part for damages incurred, and if Ross would change his smug attitude and stay out of trouble in Georgia, his juvenile record would be clean. I held my breath and silently prayed that Ross wouldn't make any snide remark; he replied that he would stay out of trouble. I wrote a check as requested and thanked the detective profusely for his time and understanding. He wished Ross well, and we were done.

With God's grace and mercy, Ross managed to stay out of trouble for the next couple of days. We moved him back to Georgia and back to his former friends at Oconee County High School. He seemed really happy to be moving back. I decided to remain in Pennsylvania for the next month until we closed on our new house in Georgia and were able to move in. I felt like I needed the time to tie- up some loose ends. Besides, it was Steve's turn to deal with Ross for a while.

I looked forward to the move back to Georgia. Things had changed, as they always do, in the years we had been gone from Pennsylvania. Since my two best friends were working full-time and had developed new friendships, I didn't get to spend much time with them. It would also be nice having our family living closer together. And as they say, the grass is always greener on the other side.

It certainly didn't take long for Ross's grass to turn brown.

CHAPTER 33

November 2004

The months following our move back to Georgia could only be described as turbulent. Ross had become more distant throughout the summer and his angry outbursts had escalated. As 2004 progressed, so did the animosity between him and Jameson; their relationship had crumbled. They had not been close for some time, but it had reached the point of near loathing. They were extremely jealous of each other; each was convinced the other received preferential treatment. Ross knew that Jameson garnered attention due to his health problems, and Jameson felt that Ross received too much undeserved attention. There were hard feelings between the two and almost constant bickering and belittling when they were together.

Since Jameson was older, he at times attempted to wield his authority; that did not bode well with Ross, at all. We emphasized to Jameson that he was Ross's brother, not his father, and he should never try to discipline him. In fact, Ross seemed to be having problems with almost everyone. Between his arguments with Steve and his disagreements with his girlfriend, Emily (whom he had maintained a long-distance relationship with while living in Pennsylvania), our house sometimes resembled a small war zone.

Speaking of our house, we had bought and moved into a small, ninety year old farmhouse. I had been in love with the house since moving back to Georgia in the late 1990s. Back then, I would drive past it several times a week when transporting Ross to and from school. Much to Steve's dismay, it had gone up for sale while we were house hunting during our latest move. I had pleaded my case long enough that Steve finally caved, and the house became ours. I repeat—I loved that house!

And then there was Ross, breaking window panes out of French doors, knocking holes in more walls (with both inanimate objects and with various body parts), and breaking numerous objects, such as his cell phone. During one very stupid episode with Steve, he smashed his electric guitar and part of his drum set. His behavior was so uncontrollable at times that on several occasions he had taken off unannounced and driven to see Emily, who was away at college. These occurrences happened both on the weekends and during the week, which of course involved skipping school.

Things progressed to the point where Steve and I went so far as to contact a school in South Carolina that rehabilitated delinquent teenagers. We were so desperate for Ross to have an attitude adjustment that we went and toured the facility one day while Ross was in school. We had gone with the intention of doing all of the necessary admission paperwork. But after taking the grand tour, talking with administration, and meeting some of the kids there, we both had a change of heart. We felt that, yes, Ross was almost uncontrollable at times and definitely needed an attitude adjustment, but we didn't feel that he deserved such as harsh an environment as would have been provided there.

Also, it was a policy of the school that, if a student attempted to run away, they would be transferred immediately to a sister facility in Jamaica. I felt pretty certain that would be Ross's ultimate destiny. I definitely didn't think that would be a good scenario.

We did use the situation to our advantage, though. We informed Ross of our initial plans; I think he was actually taken aback by it. And whenever we needed any kind of leverage when dealing with our adorable son, we would hold the threat of sending him away over his head. I'm sure it sounds callous, but it did seem to make him stop and think, and compose himself from time to time.

After the road trip Steve and I went on, things became a little calmer at home. There were still arguments and tense moments, especially towards Ross's nonchalant attitude towards schoolwork. But his overall behavior had shown improvement.

Then things got interesting. Steve and I were invited to join two couples, who we were friends with in Pennsylvania, for a weekend in North Carolina. We were more than a little hesitant to leave Ross home alone, but he *was* doing better, and we'd only be gone forty-eight hours. I know you're probably thinking how dumb we were. We thought the same thing, but a little break was just too tempting. Besides, it would be good to see old friends.

Our drive to North Carolina was very pleasant, and then we spent a nice evening catching up with our friends.

At about three in the morning, my cell phone rang—it was Ross. By the sound of his voice I could tell he was upset, even though I was still half asleep.

"I've lost Otto," he whined. He sounded on the verge of tears.

"What do you mean, you've lost Otto?" I questioned.

By now I was fully awake and beginning to get unsettled. Otto was our little Cairn terrier (like Toto from *The Wizard of Oz*) . He was cute but not terribly smart. He also had a tendency to run away when he got the chance.

Ross continued, "I didn't think he had gotten out, but I've called him and called him and looked all around, but I can't find him. I've even driven all around calling him."

Otto being missing at 3:00 a.m. was not a good thing, but what was I to do? I certainly wasn't going to get up and drive six hours home.

"Drive around and look for him one more time," I instructed, "then just wait till morning and look some more. You're probably not going to be able to spot him in the dark."

"Okay," he objectively responded.

"I love you, Ross," I said.

"Love you, too," he replied.

As I laid back down, I thought what a great way to spoil a nice weekend. I was worried about Otto; we might not ever see him again.

Approximately fifteen minutes later, my phone rang again; it was a much lighter-sounding Ross on the other end.

"I found Otto," he announced. "He was in my closet."

I thought it strange that Otto was hiding in the closet; I didn't remember him ever doing that before. Oh well, I was glad he had been found. I reminded Ross to make certain the front and backdoors were both closed tightly, and we said our good-byes. I was back asleep in an instant.

After breakfast, we all had just left our friends' house to go ride around and see the sights. My cell phone rang. Good grief, what now? It wasn't Ross. It was the mother of one of Ross's friends. She started the conversation by apologizing for bothering me on a Saturday morning. She wanted to know if I was at home. I briefly explained where we were; she wasn't surprised to find out that we were out of town.

She went on to relate how her son, Matt, had told her he was going to spend the night at Ross's house the previous night. She explained that she had been having some trouble with Matt, so she decided to drive by my house to make certain Matt's car was there. She said she drove by at around midnight, and there were cars parked everywhere in my yard.

This information didn't come as a shock to me. We often had a lot of extra teenagers at our house on the weekends, partly due to the fact that a converted garage on our property made an excellent cottage to hang out in. I relayed this to Lillian. She acknowledged the fact, then she reiterated that there had been a lot of cars at my house; they were parked all the way to the road.

Oh, that would have been a lot of cars, considering our house sat a good 100 yards back from the road. I thanked Lillian for her call and made sure she knew I really appreciated her concern. I then relayed the story to Steve and our friends. We concluded it must have been some kind of party at my house; no wonder Otto had been hiding! We would deal with it when we got home. We were going to enjoy the rest of the weekend with our friends; and we did.

Upon arriving home on Sunday night, everything appeared very quiet. Ross's car was also gone. Nothing seemed out of sorts. Then we walked into the house; it really did resemble a war zone. Dirty dishes filled the kitchen sink and the countertops. The floor was nasty. From the kitchen I could see into Ross's bedroom—it was a disaster. As we moved from the kitchen into the den, I stopped in my tracks. It looked as if there was a layer of ash covering everything in the den—the furniture, the hardwood floor, the mantle- and then I spotted Abby.

Abby, our lovely, oversized, mahogany sable- colored sheltie, was sitting patiently in the middle of the room waiting for us. And she was a mess! I went over to rub her, and discovered she had syrup all in her beautiful fur. There was also syrup on the coffee table, on the rug, and all over the front door.

Steve was on the phone in an instant calling Ross. "Where are you!" he demanded.

Ross replied that he had gone to see Emily and that he was on his way back home.

"You better get home now!" was Steve's response.

After I had gotten over my shock of seeing Abby, I walked into my bedroom. My bed was in an upheaval, but what was on my bed caught my attention even more. My entire bed was covered with pictures, and plates, and cups and saucers, and wall racks, and wall decorations. It then hit me that nothing had been hanging on any of the walls as I had left it on Friday. I later learned that Ross had taken everything off of the walls and had locked the objects in my bedroom so nothing would get broken. Of course, since he locked the bedroom door, he had to break the lock on a window in order to get back into the bedroom and unlock the door. Good intentions, but not well thought out.

Ross, after arriving home, somewhat pieced together the weekend's events for us. Remember that list I mentioned a while back? Well, take a guess at another one of the items on it. If you said, *Throw* a *keg party*, you'd be right. Since he was going to be home alone for the weekend, he decided to throw the party of the century, just because he could.

Apparently, things got a little out of hand. According to Ross, he didn't intend on actually having kegs of beer at the shindig, but once word of the party got out, an uncontrollable number of people showed up, including college students bearing gifts of beer kegs. Ross swore he didn't even know half of the people who attended. All I know is that they made a mess and that I was so thankful that no one was injured in any way, and that no neighbors called the police.

I even had an elderly neighbor tell me the next morning that he wouldn't have known there had even been a party had people not thrown beer bottles and cans over the fence into his backyard. He did kindly ask that the mess be removed, which we did in a timely manner. I also voiced my sincerest apologies to him.

Of course, true to Ross's charming nature, he tried to tell Steve and me that the entire incident was *our* fault. He said we should have known better than to leave him alone for a weekend (he got that right!). He also proceeded to tell us that we should have thanked him for taking everything off of the walls to keep them from being broken. And for he and his friends cleaning the house for us. And that we should really appreciate his friend Matt (remember Matt?), because he did his best to keep things from becoming more out of control than they already were. He also assured us that we wouldn't have to worry about him ever having another keg party—that was crossed off of his list. Besides, he added, it was too much work.

We eventually determined the ash covering the den was caused from the vacuum cleaner somehow blowing out debris instead of sucking it in. We never did solve the syrup mystery.

Ross really didn't enjoy his punishment, but he thought it was all worth it in the end.

Would he feel that way the next time?

CHAPTER 34

December 2004

Although Ross was now attending school on a fairly regular basis, only missing a day here and there, it was very apparent that he had a strong disliking for the place. He routinely verbalized how much he hated it and what a waste of time it was.

Some of his grades reflected his sentiment, especially math. Mathematics had always been one of his weaker subjects, but neglecting to turn in homework assignments was killing his average. His attitude was so poor that he would even refrain from turning in homework that he had completed. I believe in part this was done simply to annoy the teacher. It didn't seem to matter to him that he was only hurting himself.

Fortunately, the high school had a computer program where parents could go online and view their student's grades, in any of their classes. I utilized this system at least daily, that's how I knew how much trouble Ross was in. He was already working with a good math tutor, but he continued to dig his own grave. Unaware of anything else I could do, I scheduled a meeting with his math teacher. It was getting close to the end of the semester, and I was desperate. The thought of Ross failing his class and having to repeat math in his very last semester of high school was more than I could bear.

When Steve and I met with the math teacher (yes, I made Steve accompany me), she was very blunt. She told us she didn't see any way possible that Ross could pass the class. She stated that he had done it to himself. He had been given plenty of opportunity to bring his grades up, but apparently he had chosen not to. I felt ill. I realized everything she was saying was true, but I could not stand to go through another math class!

In a moment of desperation, I blurted out, "If I thought it would do any good, I would bribe you to pass him." There were several other staff members present for the meeting; everyone just kind of looked at me. I could feel my face turning crimson. I attempted to lighten the mood by doing a little laugh and saying something to the effect of, "I really wouldn't do that." But boy, oh boy, if I had thought bribery would have bought Ross a nice passing grade, I would have been writing that check!

As we were leaving the school, Steve shook his head, chuckled, and said, "I can't believe you just bribed a teacher!"

"I did not bribe a teacher," I retorted, "I said I would bribe her if it would do any good."

"Same thing," he replied.

For the remaining few weeks of the semester, I stayed on Ross's back to do his work. Gradually, his math grade began to rise. During the last week and a half before finals were administered, I made certain he visited his math tutor on a daily basis. How did I know he actually went every day? Funny you should ask.

I had received a call early one afternoon from the high school nurse. She stated that Ross was in her office, complaining of feeling sick, and that he wanted to go home. I would have to give permission for him to leave. She then went on to explain that the parking lot guard had brought Ross to her office after catching him attempting to leave the school grounds without a pass.

When I heard this, I was pretty much certain that Ross wasn't actually sick—he was scheming. The nurse then proceeded to tell me that Ross was very insistent on going home. All sorts of red flags popped up inside my head.

A. I knew he had math class in the afternoon.
B. I was almost certain he was faking.
C. He was probably headed for a meltdown.

The nurse asked if I would like to speak to Ross. Honestly, no, I didn't want to talk to him, but I felt as though I needed to try and calm him down. It would be similar to diffusing a bomb. When he got on the phone, he was very insistent on coming home, and I could tell his mood was escalating.

I tried to calmly explain to him that he didn't need to come home; he definitely needed to go to math class. Me telling him no, of course, made matters worse. The tone and volume of his voice were growing stronger. He insisted that He Needed To Come Home! I assured him that no, he didn't.

Then he tried a different approach.

"Just let me come home."

"Why?"

"I need to poop."

"So go to the bathroom and poop."

"I can't do it at school."

"I guess if you have to go bad enough you will." "Just let me come home! You're making it worse!" "How am I making it worse?" "You're causing me to get into trouble!"

"I didn't tell you to try and leave school without permission." "You're just making it worse!"

"Ross, you are staying at school. Let me speak with the nurse again." After I finished my conversation with the nurse and hung up, I had mixed emotions. I actually felt a little sorry for Ross. He had almost begged me to give him permission to come home, in a crazy teenage sort of way. And I had come close to giving in. On the other hand, after all of the grief he had put me through for the past several months, let him suffer through the rest of the afternoon at school.

But alas, the joke was on me. Shortly after hanging up the phone, I received a second call from the school. This time it was the assistant principal. She called to inform me that because of Ross's attempt to leave school property without permission, he would have his school parking permit revoked for thirty school days. He wasn't allowed to drive his car or anyone else's car to school for that time period. I was told I would be receiving an official letter in the mail.

Oh, good! Now I would either have to drive him to and from school every day or trust one of his friends to transport him. And because of all of the Christmas holidays, and several other holidays being celebrated in January, Ross wouldn't be allowed to drive back to school until almost February.

And that's how I know that he actually went to tutoring each afternoon—I drove him there. And the story about needing to relieve himself of bodily waste was a total fabrication. He and a friend had decided that they would both leave school and meet for a Mexican meal. The friend apparently got away with it. Ross ate his Mexican meal after school officially let out for the day. He also paid me back by not returning home from school until after 9:00 p.m. (and not answering his cell phone during the unaccounted for time). We had quite a few tense days for a while, but we got over it. We always did.

Oh, and as for math, he made a 93 on his final. He passed the class with a solid C. Ross could at times be much smarter intellectually than he professed to be.

CHAPTER 35

January 2005

A new year, which meant the final semester of Ross's high school career. Christmas break had been pleasant; we had enjoyed a nice family Christmas. Since this was Ross's last semester, he had managed to hold his complaints to a minimum.

But, there was trouble on the dating front.

He and Emily had pretty much been an item since the summer of 2003. They had been able to maintain an eight hundred mile long-distance relationship for approximately eight months when we had moved back to Pennsylvania. But since Emily had gone off to college, it seemed that seventy miles was tearing them apart. Ross had driven over to campus for the evening so the two of them could talk.

Sometime between nine and nine thirty, we got a phone call from Ross, and he did not sound happy. As it turned out, he was in a small town about twenty minutes away from our house, and he had just received a speeding ticket. He had been clocked going eighty-four miles an hour in a forty-five mile an hour zone. He was going how fast?

He tried to explain that he and Emily had broken up, and he was driving so fast because he just wanted to get home. We cautioned him to drive the speed limit the remainder of the way. We would discuss the details when he got home.

When Ross arrived home, he was visibly shaken. We weren't certain if it was due to the break up or because of the ticket or both. We kept our cool and asked Ross to explain what happened. He repeated what he had told us over the phone. Then he explained that he had just turned onto the city bypass, he realized he was in the final stretch home, and he just drove. He thought the speed limit on that section of the highway was 55mph. The next thing he knew, he saw flashing blue lights behind him and he was being pulled over. He commented that the cop was a smart ass.

Oh, no, I thought to myself. "You didn't mouth off at him, did you?" I pleadingly asked.

"No, I did not," he replied.

After he finished relaying the details of the story, we told him we were sorry to hear about him and Emily, and then we said we'd wait to see what the next step should be. After Ross went to his room to listen to some music and to de-stress, Steve and I just looked at each other. Then I sighed, "Oh great!"

Ironically, we had been through a similar situation a few years earlier when Jameson had received a large speeding citation while driving through a very small town at night. We basically knew what to expect; the fine would be hefty, and if we didn't want this to remain on Ross's record, we would need the help of an attorney. And, thanks to Jameson, we were acquainted with a good lawyer.

As I previously stated, we knew the fine would be hefty. But when Ross received the official paperwork through the mail a couple of days later, I thought my brain had forgotten how to read. The ticket could not possibly have said $450.00! I had never heard of a speeding ticket costing that much! On top of that, Ross was required to appear before the judge in order to see if he would be allowed to keep his license. And we were paying a nice chunk of change to retain a lawyer.

Friends told us that Ross would learn his lesson if Steve and I didn't do anything to help him out of his mess. They might have been right. Then, on the other hand, they didn't know Ross nearly as well as his parents did. He was a very slow learner when it came to learning a lesson. Besides, Steve and I didn't want him to have a driving record. Ross did have his faults, but he had proven to be a good driver.

So, we ignored our friends' advice, hired the lawyer, and paid the traffic fine. The lawyer was able to speak with the judge and persuade him to allow Ross to keep his driver's license, contingent on Ross performing three tasks.

1. He had to attend a defensive driving class.
2. He had to perform twenty hours of community service.
3. He had to write an essay entitled "Privileges of Driving" and give it to the judge for approval. He was allowed sixty days to complete the assignments.

The defensive driving class was fairly pain-free, although he did have to get out of bed early and waste an entire Saturday. Completing the community service was a bit trickier since he could only work at it for a short while after school in the afternoons and on Saturdays. He decided to help out at the local animal shelter—visions of playing with puppies and kittens danced in his head. As it turned out, he wasn't even allowed to touch the animals; he did a lot of grunt work. But he didn't voice too many complaints, and he completed all of his required hours.

Writing the essay turned out to be the real bone of contention. That assignment really brought out his defiant streak. After much complaining, griping, and procrastination, the essay was finally written. It was then taken to the lawyer in order to be delivered to the judge. Since I had to constantly remind him to work on the essay, I felt as though I had done more work than Ross.

In the end, the judge did allow Ross to keep his license, and he didn't even have to make an appearance in court. I was greatly relieved at that turn of events, because Ross's appearance at that stage in his life could not be called courtroom worthy. His hair was past his shoulders, he had a lip ring in his lower lip, and he exuded a rather strong "don't care" attitude. But, despite his more undesirable traits, he still had one killer of a smile.

That smile melted my heart, and saved his hide, on more than one occasion.

CHAPTER 36

February 2005

After what seemed like a very brief truce, Steve and Ross were into arguing hot and heavy, again. It appeared as though they couldn't even be in the same room together without becoming angry at each other. Anything set them off, no matter how stupid or insignificant it seemed.

I felt like I was always being the referee between the two of them. And I often wondered which one was supposed to be the adult. A lot of times it was like breaking up an argument between two children.

The constant battling and subsequent stress that arose from it also definitely put a strain on my relationship with Steve. Ironically, everything that we went through with Jameson seemed to bond us more closely together, as a couple and as parents. Now that bond was coming unglued.

After living through our trauma and heartache with Jameson, mine and Steve's personalities also kind of did a somersault. Steve had always been a very laid back, easy going type of person. It took a lot to ruffle his feathers. I had always been relatively easy going also, but I was much more critical of people and situations than he was. I saw everything as either black or white, no grey areas allowed. Steve could always adjust more easily to moral or ethical situations.

Abracadabra! I had turned into the one who could go with the flow and not sweat the small stuff, while Steve seemed to worry about everything and became uptight at the slightest inclination.

I contribute part of my personality change to experiencing Ross as a teenager. I lived with him through all of his fads—mohawk hair, purple hair, shoulder length hair, halfway down his back hair, lip piercings, painted fingernails, grungy clothes, worn out clothes and shoes, studded belts and wristbands, long tube socks(worn with shorts), wild T-shirts, skintight jeans. You get the picture.

When in public, I noticed how people would look at him. Only I knew that the inner Ross didn't always match the outer Ross. For all of our difficult, estranged periods, we also had really enjoyable times together. We both enjoyed eating out at various restaurants, so when Steve would be out of town, Ross and I would take turns choosing where to eat. We also had very interesting conversations during these meals. Ross actually did most of the talking. He would enlighten me on the topics that held his current interest. No matter how out there the subject matter was, it was always nice to see him become animated over a favorite subject. So when I would see wild, scary looking teenagers, instead of jumping to conclusions and thinking the worst of them, I began reminding myself that they were someone's child. And I wondered if they enjoyed having a meal with their mom, or playing music trivia each time they listened to the radio together.

Yes, Ross had helped me to learn patience and to be less condemning, but he and Steve could still drive me crazy! I had gradually learned that when Ross was angry or upset, it was best just to leave him alone for a while so he could calm down. It was then much easier to carry on a civil conversation with him.

Steve apparently was a very slow learner. I could not get the aforementioned concept across to him. If Ross was mad or upset, Steve would continue to badger him until all hell broke loose. That was exactly what had happened one particular night, when their argument escalated into a full-fledged smackdown. There had been yelling, things thrown, things broken, threats made, ultimatums, physical contact, and crying (mine). It ended with Ross storming out of the house and going to spend the night at his friend Aaron's house.

After Ross stormed out and drove off into the night, the battle continued, but it was now between Steve and me. He was mad because I didn't back him up one hundred percent. I was upset not only that Ross felt the need to leave, but I was afraid of what he might do next. When he was in that frame of mind, he didn't think clearly nor make good decisions. I sincerely thought he might leave town. I mean, we didn't even know if he had actually gone to Aaron's house.

His cell phone had gotten broken in the ruckus, so I couldn't call to check on him (he probably wouldn't have answered his phone anyway). I really didn't want to phone Aaron's house because it was well after midnight, and I didn't want to disturb the entire household. But I *had* to find out if he was there and safe for the night.

After much debate, I decided to drive over to Aaron's house. I just wanted to make certain Ross's car was there. On the drive over, I kept worrying about what would happen if Ross did decide to actually run away. I wouldn't put it past him to just up and leave during the middle of the night.

When I arrived at Aaron's, I was relieved to see Ross's car parked on the road in front of the house. At least he was where he said he would be. Then panic again swept over me. I had to make certain he didn't up and leave. I turned my headlights off and parked in front of his car. I sat there in the dark deciding what to do. There was no traffic on the road, and Aaron's house sat a little ways away from other houses.

Suddenly, I knew what I had to do. I fumbled through my glove compartment and found a multipurpose tool which contained a wire cutter. I got out of my van, quietly closed my door, and crept over to Ross's car. Luckily, I was able to open his hood without much trouble. I felt like a cat burglar, creeping around in the dark in the middle of the night. But I was a woman on a mission; a mother protecting her child.

I stared down at the car's engine, illuminated by the moonlight. I didn't know a spark plug from a fuel line, but I did know what the battery was. And I knew if something was wrong with the battery, then the car wouldn't run. I felt around beside the battery until my hand fell upon a small cable that appeared to be connected to it. I took a deep breath, said a little prayer, and cut the cable.

I didn't really know what I had cut, or to what extent I had damaged the car, but I was pretty certain that the car wouldn't be able to crank. Therefore, Ross wouldn't be able to make any type of getaway. I looked around to make certain I had not been seen, and then quietly closed the hood. I got back into my car and drove home.

After returning home, I laid awake in bed hatching out the rest of my scheme. Then I waited for morning.

I wanted to be back at Aaron's early, before Ross had a chance to discover his car wouldn't crank and then possibly become enraged. I arrived around seven, about the time the boys would be getting up for school. I went into the house to thank Aaron's mom for allowing Ross to sleepover, and then she went into the basement to let him know I was there. When he appeared he was quiet and subdued.

I explained to him that I had come over in order to make certain he was going to school. I then suggested he get ready at home so he could change into clean clothes. He agreed. We said our good-byes to Aaron and his mom, and then Ross got into his car. It wouldn't crank. He tried several times, but no luck. He said it had been running fine the night before.

I could tell he was beginning to become agitated, so I suggested we just leave his car and we would worry about it later. Ross wasn't very happy with that plan, but he agreed to it. I explained that I would have it towed to a garage later in the day and they could take a look at it. He continued to insist that the car had been running fine the day before; I continued to play dumb.

When I met the wrecker service at Aaron's later in the morning, I continued my charade and I lied through my teeth. When the wrecker driver looked under the hood, he could tell immediately that the problem was a cut cable. He asked if my son had been having any problems with anyone who would have done that to his car. I feigned ignorance and said it was probably just a random act. He then recommended that I notify the police. I told him I didn't think it was necessary, but I assured him I would tell the owners of the house what had happened.

The tow truck driver's departing remark to me was that whoever messed with the car had sure done a good job of it. I felt a certain sense of pride at my accomplishment. Yeah, I had to pay a nice little amount to have the car repaired.

But for once, I had pulled one over on Ross.

CHAPTER 37

March 27, 2005

Life continued along its stressful little course. Ross had good days and bad days. The occasional good days, I truly enjoyed his company. The bad days, I walked on eggshells. I never knew when something would set him off and he would explode. Even during his worst outbursts, I had finally learned to keep *my* anger under control.

In fact, Ross had this uncanny way of causing me to calm down. It was really nothing that he did or didn't do, and I honestly could never explain it. I could be so mad at him that I wanted nothing to do with him. Then, after even briefly talking with him, my anger would subside. It was the strangest thing. In my mind, I would have an elaborate speech planned out, ready to nail him to the wall (metaphorically). Then, poof! I wouldn't recite a third of my intended speech. It was a very annoying scenario each time it happened.

To compound my frustration, I was in a deep sense of denial. Steve and I both had turned into those parents who, instead of acting responsibly and taking charge of the situation, had chosen to look the other way and pretend certain things weren't taking place. I'm not sure if we were so emotionally worn -out that we just didn't care anymore, or we were afraid that if we took our blinders off, things might even be worse than we realized.

It was Easter weekend. Other than Steve's mom and his grandmother, his family wasn't very attuned to attending church. But it just so happened, this particular year, everyone had planned on attending Easter services with Steve's mom. Because there were going to be so many people staying at her house for the weekend, we had decided not to go until Saturday afternoon.

On Saturday morning, Ross had begun complaining about not being home on Saturday night. He complained that there wouldn't be anything to do at Grandmama's house, and he wanted to be at home to hang out with his friends that night. He said he could drive over on Sunday morning (Steve's mom lived about two and a half hours from us). I knew there would be a slim chance of that happening. I also knew more than likely he and his friends wanted to get together and smoke pot (one of those "look the other way" items).

Steve was very adamant about all of us going together on Saturday afternoon, but I had begun to give in. I knew if we forced Ross to go, he would be unbearable to be around. I finally talked Steve into him and Jameson going on ahead, and I would wait and go with Ross the following morning, just to make certain he went.

Our farmhouse had a detached garage on the property that had been converted into a cottage. This was Ross's refuge and weekend hangout. This was where band practice took place, where lazy Saturday movie watching occurred, and where Ross's friends slept on the weekends.

On the night before Easter, only one friend slept over. I told Ross I would wake them up at seven o'clock the next morning, and he and I would be on the road by seven thirty. I also told him to go to bed at a decent time; I didn't want him grumpy all day due to lack of sleep.

On Sunday morning, I didn't have much trouble getting him out of bed, and we were on the road by seven forty-five. It didn't take Ross long to make himself comfortable in the passenger seat and fall asleep. He slept soundly throughout the entire trip.

When we arrived at Steve's mom's, Ross went around and told everyone hello, and then he disappeared into the back bedroom. A few minutes before time for everyone to leave for church, I went back to the bedroom to tell him it was time to go. I found him in the bed sleeping.

When I awakened him and told him to get up, he said he didn't feel good. I responded by telling him he had probably stayed up too late, and he could take a nap after lunch.

He again told me he didn't feel good and he didn't want to go to church. Well, that certainly came as no surprise. He seldom attended church with us anymore, but we had discussed his going on Easter as a family group and he had agreed to go. I asked him again to get up and let's go.

"No!" he emphatically replied. "I'm not going. I just want to be left alone so I can sleep."

By now I was becoming extremely exasperated. "Get out of the bed *now*!" I hissed.

Ross just laid there like a slug.

About that time Steve entered the room and asked what was going on. I told him that Ross was refusing to get out of bed and go to church with the whole family. Now it was Steve's turn to lose his cool, and boy, did he ever! He began ranting and raving and, what he did best, making threats. Ross and I, along with his friend David and my parents, had plans to leave for Disney World in a couple of days for Spring Break. Steve was promising Ross that if he didn't get up and go to church, the trip was off.

Ross was unfazed. He simply didn't care what the consequences might be. He was not going to church.

I had to get Steve out of the house before he had a stroke. We decided to go ahead and meet the rest of the family at church, and just leave Ross to himself. But when we arrived at church, I couldn't stand the thought of Steve's mom being disappointed.

She had assured us back at the house that it was all right if Ross didn't attend.

But it wasn't all right with me. Ross had never acted disrespectful to any of his grandparents or to any other adults for that matter. Sure, he had treated me and Steve like dirt on several occasions, but not others. And despite what Steve's mom had said, I was sure she was somewhat disappointed that Ross wasn't a part of her family Easter.

I encouraged Steve to go on into church while I went back to try one more time to persuade Ross to do the right thing. On the short drive back, I was praying that his conscience had caused him to have a change of heart. No such luck.

When I walked into the house, Ross was out of the bed, but he appeared very agitated. I asked him if he was awake enough now to go to church. He replied with a resounding, "I'm not going. Just leave me alone."

I attempted once again to explain to him how important I felt it was for all of us to go to church with Grandmama this one time. He was unwavering. In fact, he became more agitated, and I became more angry. I launched an assault on him. I told him how selfish he was and how he didn't care about anyone's feelings but his own.

The conversation turned into a yelling match. We were both out of control and screaming things that we really didn't mean. Although, on some level, the hurtful words felt good to me as I said them.

Then Ross's focus turned to threatening to kill himself. I wasn't alarmed; this hand had been played before. There was a pocketknife lying on the top of the television. Ross grabbed it and said, "I think I'll stab myself right now!"

Out of my mouth immediately came, "No, wait a minute! If you really want to kill yourself, let's get a knife that'll really do the job!" I stormed into the kitchen, rifled through one of the drawers, and walked back into the living room with a large carving knife.

"This should do it," I announced.

"What the...," he mumbled in a completely astonished voice.

Uh oh, I thought to myself. I knew I had gone too far.

In a flash, Ross had grabbed Steve's car keys off of the table and was out the door. I ran after him, but by the time I reached the car he had already cranked it and locked the doors. As I stood in the driveway yelling for him to get out, he backed into the road and headed down the street.

I ran back into the house and grabbed my cell phone. I called his phone, hoping he had it with him and would answer it. He picked up on the third ring.

"Where are you going?" I beseeched.

"I might just go find a big tree and crash the car into it. That would make you happy, wouldn't it?" was his reply.

I could feel myself on the verge of crying. "No, that would not make me happy. And your daddy would kill both of us if you wrecked his car," I somberly retorted.

"Please come back to the house," I persuaded.

"I might go crash this car, or I may just drive a while," he coolly responded.

"I'll see you in a bit?" I asked hopefully.

"Probably," he replied.

After about twenty minutes, Ross returned to the house. Both he and the car were in one piece. As he walked through the living room, I said, "I love you, son. You know that."

"I know," he replied, "now I'm going to sleep."

When everyone returned from church, I explained that Ross wasn't feeling well and I had decided to stay home with him. Of course, Steve's mom was only concerned with the fact that he wasn't feeling well. I was glad about that. I was feeling down because of the morning's events, but I was also disheartened because I had missed Easter services. As far as I could remember, I had never missed an Easter Sunday at church before.

Despite my low spirits and the morning's fiasco, we all had a nice, big lunch together except, of course, for Ross, who slept throughout the entire afternoon. Late in the day, I was finally able to arouse him from his slumber. He could at least grace everyone with his presence for a short while.

Of course, his grandmama was babying him because he was "sick." She also assured him that it had been okay for him to stay home from church since he wasn't feeling well. I played along with the sick charade. By now I had concluded that Ross had probably stayed up late smoking pot, but I certainly didn't want the entire family to become aware of it.

One family member was savvy enough not to buy into the illness hoax. Steve's nephew had been involved with drugs when he was younger. He had taken Steve aside and suggested that Ross's erratic behavior was due to some drug other than marijuana. He also strongly recommended that we try to find out what that drug was and do whatever possible to prevent it from becoming a habit.

Steve was extremely grateful for his nephew's input. As a matter of fact, on the drive home, we made the decision to take Ross straight to the crisis center at our local hospital when we arrived back in town. Steve and Jameson were riding together; Ross was sound asleep in the backseat of my car. Steve was able to call ahead to the center and make the arrangements to take him there.

We realized it was going to be difficult to do, and we feared Ross would never forgive us for taking him. But we felt it was something we had to do, for Ross's sake and for his well-being. I worried the rest of the way home about how Ross would react, and how long he would hate us.

The crisis center personnel had instructed Steve to call them when we were about ten minutes from arriving. They cautioned that Ross would probably be very resistant to what was taking place and might refuse to get out of the car. They would have a security guard waiting on us to usher Ross inside. I had made the decision not to awaken him until we had arrived at the hospital, for fear of him jumping out of the car if he knew what was happening.

As we approached the hospital, I felt sick. I hated that we were being so devious, but I hated even worse the thought that Ross might be involved in some really hard core drug use. Steve and I couldn't just sit by and wait to see what happened.

When I stopped in front of the hospital entrance, I called for Ross to wake up. I could see the guard approaching the car. Oh, I just wanted all of this to go away and for us to have our happy family life of years past. But this was reality, and I had to be strong. As Ross was stirring in the backseat, I called again for him to wake up. Then I told him we were at the hospital, and that he needed to be checked out.

About the moment the guard opened the car door, a look of recognition crossed Ross's face; he understood why we were there. He got out of the car, cursing and telling the guard not to touch him—he could go in without any help. And the way he looked at Steve and me could only be described as a look of betrayal. Jameson wanted to stay with us and be supportive, but we felt it would be better if he took

Steve's car and went home. Since he and Ross weren't the closest of brothers, we didn't want Ross having hard feelings toward Jameson for taking part in the deception.

While Ross was going through the admission process, Steve and I were told we'd have to remain in the waiting area. Ross would go through a brief admission Q&A, have blood drawn for a drug screen, and meet with the counselor on call. After all of that was completed, one of us could go and wait with him until the therapist had evaluated everything. Then all four of us would meet together to discuss a plan of action.

While we were sitting in the waiting area, we both agreed that we had done what was necessary, no matter how disheartened we felt. As we were sitting there consoling each other, our pastor, Brother Crist, appeared. My initial thoughts were: how did he know we were there, and did he know why we were there.

As our conversation began, we learned that he was at the ER with an ill family member. Steve likewise said that Ross had become sick on our way home from out of town. I couldn't believe we were sitting there lying to our preacher, but we just couldn't bring ourselves to tell him the truth. What type of family would he think he'd been pastoring all of these years?

After a while, a nurse came to take one of us back to see Ross. Steve urged that I go; he would continue to visit with Brother Crist. When I walked into the exam room where Ross was, he smirked, "I hope you're happy. I told you to just let me sleep and I'd be fine."

"You're not fine," I solemnly replied.

Our conversation was strained, but it continued to flow. Ross admitted to staying up until four thirty in the morning on Saturday night and experimenting with cocaine. He wouldn't say where he got the cocaine. He did say that his friend who was with him the previous night wasn't involved with it and repeatedly tried to talk him out of using it. Ross also acknowledged that he had ingested an extremely large amount of cocaine, and that he would never use it again. He said he hated the way it made him feel.

I was now overwhelmed even more so than before. I was shocked to hear him say that he had used cocaine. Using marijuana was bad enough, but didn't he realize how dangerously addictive cocaine could be? Didn't he value his life, and his future, more than that? Then, to apparently add insult to injury, Ross informed me that he had told the therapist that I had encouraged him to kill himself that morning by handing him a knife. Oh great, now they're going to want to ship both of us off to rehab!

After waiting a while longer, all three of us were reunited to meet with the therapist. He told us news we already knew: Ross had traces of marijuana and cocaine in his system. He told us news we were happy to hear: he didn't believe Ross was a suicide risk, and he thought Ross was truthful about only having used cocaine the one time. And he told us news that surprised us: he wasn't going to commit Ross to a rehab facility, but he did insist he go to counseling.

We had been there and done that with counseling, but we were willing to try it again, especially if it would keep him out of rehab and in school. The therapist gave us a list of a few counselors to choose from. He also told us that during their initial conversation, Ross had mentioned the Disney trip that was being cancelled. The therapist strongly suggested that we continue with the trip as planned. He thought cancelling it would probably do more harm than good, seeing that it was something positive that Ross was really excited about. Steve and I questioned the therapist's suggestion, but he held firm to his recommendation.

Disney World, here we come?

CHAPTER 38

April 1, 2005

In light of our Easter extravaganza, I was understandably apprehensive about our trip to Disney World. The therapist at the hospital crisis center had felt it would be for the best to go as planned. But the therapist wouldn't be going on the trip with us, now would he? I had decided to take his advice and hope for the best. Besides, if I had cancelled the trip, I wouldn't only have been hurting Ross, I would have been disappointing my parents as well. And I really hadn't wanted to go into any of the gory details with them anyway.

The trip turned out surprisingly well, aside from a couple of snafus. We drove down in separate cars; Ross and his friend David in Ross's car, and me and my parents in my van. Since the route to Florida passed right through my parents' town of Macon, I just stopped on the way and picked them up. Ross didn't want to have to drive right in front of me or behind me for the entire drive, so we checked in with each other via cell phone at frequent intervals.

We also stayed in separate hotels, so we had to arrive at approximately the same time so I could check them into their room (since they were underage). Somehow, they managed to end up in the nicer hotel; not quite sure how that happened. The original plan had been to get together for a couple of meals during our short stay, but with the crowd of people present that week, it was nearly impossible to synchronize eating schedules. Note to self: Never visit Disney World again when the Florida school systems are on spring break!

We did see Ross one time—when my van required repair work and I had to borrow his car for a couple of hours. Thank goodness Disney World had its own automotive repair center. And thank goodness my van decided to have problems while we were at Disney World instead of on the trip back home. I would've hated being stuck on the side of the road.

The morning of our departure back home, I stopped by Ross's hotel room to make certain he and David were packed and ready to go. I didn't dare step foot into the room; I didn't want to see how messy it was. Since I had to stop in Macon to take my parents back home, I reluctantly agreed not to constantly keep in touch with the boys. They were planning on making a couple of stops before leaving Orlando, and they wanted to travel at their own pace. I instructed them to call me if they ran into any trouble, and I would call them occasionally just to check-in.

My parents and I had a pleasant drive back to their house. It had been a nice get-together for the three of us. And, Ross had not posed any problems during the trip, although I had begun to feel a little twinge of anxiety. I had been unable to reach Ross on his cell phone for the past few hours. In order not to alarm my parents, I had commented how Ross had a habit of not keeping his phone charged.

As my parents and I said our good-byes and I headed toward home, the drive allowed me more time to become worried. It was true; Ross did have a tendency to let his phone battery go dead. But I couldn't help but think of other reasons why he wasn't answering his phone. What if he had been involved in a wreck? Or worse yet, what if he had taken this opportunity to run away from home? David didn't have a very good relationship with his parents; in fact, he lived at my house most of the time. What if he and Ross cooked up a scheme not to return home, now that they had the perfect opportunity to go elsewhere?

I knew I was probably letting my imagination run wild, but I had learned with Ross, anything was possible. The trip from my parents' home to my house took about an hour and a half. If Ross was headed home, I didn't even know if he was traveling ahead of me or behind me. I called Steve to see if perhaps he had heard from him. No, he hadn't.

Night had fallen. I was about forty minutes away from home, and still no contact with Ross. Just then, my cell phone rang. It was a number I didn't recognize, but I answered it anyway. On the other end was a voice I recognized immediately—Ross.

"Hey," he said nonchalantly, "where are you?"

"I'm getting close to home," I answered. "Where are you?" "How far are you from home?" he questioned.

I replied, "About forty minutes away." "Can you come get us?" he asked.

My heart dropped. Oh my God, I thought, they're in jail somewhere.

Ross continued to explain that he was calling from a pay phone. The drive from Macon to our house in Watkinsville follows a very long, dark stretch of road. There are two major intersections along the way; each of them has a convenience store located on the right-hand side. At the second intersection, you turn left onto a four-lane highway to continue on toward Watkinsville. Ross wasn't paying attention and turned left at the first intersection, onto a two-lane road; this takes you to the middle of nowhere.

After realizing his mistake, and since there were no cars in sight, he attempted to make a U-turn in the middle of the road. He probably would have been successful, except for the fact that the area had received a lot of rain over the past few days. This made the shoulder of the road extremely muddy, so much so that Ross's car became stuck. The more he attempted to break free from the mud, the more stuck he became.

I strangely felt an instant relief flow through my body. At least the two of them weren't in any serious trouble, or on the run. Ross went on to explain that his cell phone was dead (what a surprise), so he couldn't call me sooner. They waited with the car for a while to see if anyone drove by that could help them. When that didn't happen, they decided to walk back to the convenience store at the crossroads. It was already closed, but luckily there was a pay phone outside.

I told them to sit tight and I would be there as soon as I could. I couldn't help but laugh; only Ross could manage to get into a situation like that. And it wasn't the first time. He had gotten our pickup truck stuck so deeply in mud, and so far off the road, while attempting to go mud bogging, that it took a massive wrecker to free it and pull it out. The wrecker had to use every inch of its cable to even be able to reach the truck.

On another occasion, he and Aaron rode far out into the country to investigate an old burned-out barn they had heard about. While trying to find the barn on foot, Ross lost his car keys (in the dark of night). He used the light from his cell phone in an attempt to locate the keys; this in turn drained all of the power from his phone. They then had to walk approximately three miles to a friend's house in order to call Aaron's mom for help. During all of this, Steve and I were in route home from a business trip. Imagine our concern when we couldn't locate Ross at 12:30 in the morning. But our concern was minimal compared to how angry Aaron's mom was!

I phoned Steve to give him an update and to tell him I was headed back to see what I could do, although I felt like telling the boys to handle it themselves. When I reached the convenience store, the two of them appeared somewhat glad to see me. We started down the road towards Ross's car. I had the impression that it was stuck only a short distance down the road. That short distance turned out to be about a mile. And it was a very dark mile; very few stars, no bright moonlight, no streetlights.

After surveying the situation, I knew we would need to call a wrecker. There was no way that car was going to be driven out of the mud.

I had been very careful when I parked behind his car; we didn't need two stuck vehicles. As I was trying to figure out how to give the wrecker service directions to our exact location, a Ford Bronco pulled alongside of us and stopped. There was a couple inside. The driver asked if we needed help; it was apparent what the problem was. I told him I was about to phone for a wrecker, and I thanked him for stopping.

The man told me his Bronco had a four-wheel drive, and that he was pretty certain he could pull our car out of the mud. I thanked him again, but told I didn't want to take the chance of damaging his Bronco. He then insisted on helping. He parked in front of Ross's car, got out of his, and began connecting the two with a very sturdy looking chain. He explained that he had helped pull cars out of the mud on more than one occasion.

When everything was in place, he got back into his Bronco and slowly began to accelerate. His tires were spinning profusely, but nothing seemed to be happening. So he accelerated more. Now his tires were really spinning, and mud was flying everywhere. Ross's car hadn't moved. The man was undeterred. He romped down on his accelerator. Tires were whining, mud was covering everything, and Ross's car just sat there.

Finally, the nice gentleman had to surrender. He apologized for being unable to free our car from its bondage. I told him to please not apologize; I was extremely grateful for all of his trouble. He apologized again for having to give up, but he and his wife needed to get home and relieve their babysitter. I thanked him once more, and they were on their way.

Or not.

It seems like now we *did* have two stuck vehicles. I felt awful. Not only was our good Samaritan's Bronco covered in mud, it was also stuck solidly in the mud. He told me not to worry about it, that he was the one who had insisted on freeing the car from its muddy captor.

As he and I stood on the side of the road discussing who to call, a pair of headlights topped the hill in the distance. In a moment, a sheriff 's car was stopped beside us. As we explained our situation, the deputy told us not to worry; he knew someone with a wrecker who lived only a few miles away. He offered to call the man, then stay with his lights flashing until the wrecker arrived. I felt as though he was my knight in shining armor.

It didn't take long for the wrecker to find us. He first freed the good Samaritan. I insisted on paying for the entire wrecker service, but the Bronco owner wouldn't allow it. He gave the wrecker driver all of the cash that he had with him, and then he agreed to let me pay the balance. After Ross's car was freed, I also gave the wrecker owner all of the cash I had. He was then kind enough to offer to send me a bill for the remaining balance.

It had been nice to be reminded that there were still very kind, helpful people in the world. It was even nicer to finally arrive back at home. It had been a long, tiresome day.

And the weekend was just getting started.

CHAPTER 39

April 3, 2005

After arriving home from Disney World on Friday night, most of Saturday was spent catching up on laundry and relaxing as much as possible. It had been a fun few days in Florida, but the stress from the previous Easter weekend was still very much present. Sunday afternoons were not very favorable to Ross because they meant Monday morning and another week of school was fast approaching.

Ross had seemed even more sullen than usual on that particular Sunday afternoon, probably because spring break was ending. Whatever the reason, he had been very distant and short-tempered throughout the afternoon. He had stayed out in the cottage the majority of the day, but the few times he was in the house he had an argumentative air about him.

Because of his mood swings and occasional bouts of anxiety, Dr. Wells had prescribed a daily dose of Paxil for Ross to take. Unfortunately, Ross had a very negative attitude towards taking prescription medication. I would have to remind him almost daily to take it. Since his temperament could be described as a little touchy, I had gently reminded him several times during the day to take his medicine. I had also made the mistake of trying to find out why he was so agitated and angry acting.

Late in the afternoon, as he left the house and walked back out to the cottage, I followed behind him, shaking the bottle of pills and telling him he really needed to take one. After he was well inside the cottage he whirled around and snatched the bottle out of my hand.

"Thank you," I said, and started to make my way back towards the door.

"See!" he cried out.

In the same instant that I was turning back around to face him, Ross took the top off of the pill bottle, poured the entire contents into his mouth, and swallowed.

"*No!*" I yelled. But it was too late. He had taken all of the pills that were in the bottle, approximately twenty-five of them, to be exact.

"Why did you do that!" I screamed.

His reply was, "You wanted me to take my medicine, so there!" Then he stormed past me. He had his car keys in his hand.

"You can't leave!" I pleaded, and I grabbed his arm.

"Watch me," he replied, as he jerked his arm away, out of my grip, and ran to his car.

I ran after him and attempted to open his car door, but he had locked the doors. As I stood there beating on the car window with my fists, he cranked the car and backed out, and then put it in drive. I was frantic. I couldn't let him drive off in his frame of mind, especially after downing an entire bottle of antidepressants. So I jumped in front of his car. But after I saw the glaring look on his face, I decided the wise thing for me to do was to move out of his way.

He quickly accelerated the car and tore down the long gravel driveway, leaving a cloud of dust behind him. I watched as he briefly slowed at the end of the driveway, and then spun onto the two lane highway. Then he was gone out of sight.

By this time, Steve had heard all of the commotion and had come outside. I hurriedly explained to him the events that had just transpired; he was worried. I was furious. Neither of us knew exactly what effects taking that many antidepressants at one time would have on Ross. He called Ross's cell phone, but of course there was no answer. I could tell he was beginning to panic. I was just very annoyed that Ross would do something so stupid. Steve tried Ross's cell phone again—still no answer.

We decided we needed to call poison control. I made the call and gave a synopsis of the situation. The poison control operator emphasized that we needed to find Ross and get him to the ER as soon as possible. She went on to explain that an overdose could cause tachycardia (very rapid heartbeat), arrhythmias (irregular heartbeat), seizures, or kidney failure. She reiterated that we needed to find him and get him to the ER as soon as possible.

Now, my annoyance was giving way to worry, especially since we didn't know where Ross was. Steve decided to call Ross's friend Aaron, with whom Ross had taken refuge before. Fortunately, Ross had just arrived at Aaron's house. Steve explained the situation to Aaron and told him not to tell Ross that we were on our way over. He then instructed Aaron to do whatever it took to keep Ross there.

When we pulled into Aaron's driveway and Ross saw us, he immediately tried to get into his car. Aaron, along with David, was somehow able to detain him. As he broke free from the two of them, he began yelling about being tricked and they weren't his friends and how he hated all of us. He was like a wild man. He began darting from place to place. Everyone was trying to talk to him and calm him down; he was uncontrollable.

As we tried to explain to him why he needed to go to the emergency room, he remained constantly on the move. He refused to go to the hospital, citing that the last time we took him there we tried to have him committed. We attempted to reason with him by promising that he wouldn't be committed, that he needed to be treated medically in order to prevent serious health issues. He wasn't swayed.

He made a break for the house and made it onto the screened in porch—that's when Steve caught up with him. A physical fight ensued. No punches were thrown, but there was a lot of kicking and flailing and openhanded hitting going on. I was afraid that both of them would end up in the ER—Ross from overdosing and Steve from a heart attack. By now I was yelling at the top of my lungs for them to stop fighting. Miraculously, Ross wore himself out.

Steve told him that he was going to the ER one way or another, even if we had to restrain him the entire way. Both Aaron and David were trying to persuade him to go for his own good. Finally he gave up. He said he'd go in order for all of us to leave him alone.

Ross was ushered into the backseat of Steve's car, which by the way, had childproof locks on the doors, so he couldn't escape at stop signs or traffic lights. I found it hard to believe that we were on our way to a hospital with Ross, again, only one week exactly from the last visit. We had taken him to Athens Regional Hospital the prior Sunday because it was the only hospital with a crisis unit. We were taking him to St. Mary's Hospital on this excursion because it was the hospital that our insurance covered.

Steve and I worried that two ER visits in a week's time would send up a red flag in the mental health community. We believed that Ross was neither suicidal nor psychotic, but we knew our opinions probably wouldn't count for much. We just knew that all of those Paxil being ingested at one time couldn't be very healthy; Ross's physical well-being was at the top of our priority list for this particular hospital visit.

Ross had been very calm on the drive to the hospital, and he remained so once we arrived at the ER. He was checked in and taken back to a private exam room almost immediately. I had been afraid that the ER staff might be somewhat rude or flippant towards him, considering the careless situation he had put himself in. To the contrary, the attending nurses and the ER doctor were all very friendly and upbeat, and not at all condescending. Ross actually appeared somewhat relaxed, and he was pleasant.

He had an electrocardiogram (EKG) done to rule out any heart anomalies that could have been a result of the overdose. He then had to obtain a urine specimen and have blood drawn for a variety of tests to be done. An IV was started in order to provide hydration and to help flush the toxins from his kidneys. Last, but definitely not least, Ross was told the good news that he wasn't going to have his stomach pumped to help rid his body of the drugs. However, he did have to drink activated charcoal to flush out his system.

The look on his face was priceless when the first cup was given to him. The charcoal cocktail looked like motor oil—thick, black, and oily. He was instructed to drink all of it, and then he would be rewarded with a second cup. The charcoal would act as a laxative to cleanse the Paxil out of his digestive system. Luckily for Ross, the bathroom was located right across the hall from his room.

He drank, made faces, drank some more, used the toilet, made more faces, continued to drink, and made several more trips to the bathroom. His lips and mouth were as black as ink. But he didn't complain. I don't know if the reality of how stupid and dangerous his earlier stunt had been had finally sunken in, or if he was just finding the entire situation amusing, but he actually did not complain. He was in fact quite cooperative, and even chatty.

Despite the fact that the three of us were sitting in an emergency room as a result of a drug overdose, Steve and I were rather enjoying Ross's company. That was a good thing, considering we had to stay in the ER for several hours. Because of the potential risk for kidney failure, a final blood test to evaluate Ross's kidney function had to be drawn six hours after the ingestion of the drug. That meant he wasn't allowed to leave until around midnight. Fortunately, the lab results had turned out okay.

Ross's attitude and demeanor had changed from raging bull to cozy kitten. He was once again deemed to be of no threat to himself or others, but was urged to attend counseling. We were given the name and address of a counseling center, along with an appointment date and time. It was reinforced that the counseling was mandatory, and follow-ups would be made to ensure his compliance.

After leaving the hospital, Ross was starving. We made a side trip through McDonald's drive-thru, and then headed for home. David, who had practically been living at our house for the past several months, was waiting for us when we arrived. Ross had to fill him in concerning his entire hospital experience. I warned them both not to stay up too much later. Spring break was over and they *would* be on time for school the first day back. I gave Ross a hug, told him I loved him, and left them for the night.

As I lay in my bed, I thought back over the events of the past few weeks. I was mentally and emotionally exhausted. As I listened to Steve sleeping quietly beside me, I silently thanked God for once again keeping Ross safe, and I asked Him to please continue to watch over him. Then I closed my eyes to sleep. Tomorrow would be another day.

CHAPTER 40

December 2005

The entire second half of two thousand five also proved to be rather eventful, but in a much nicer manner than the first half. May 15th had been one of the most gratifying days of my life—Ross graduated from high school! Not only had he graduated, but his GPA was high enough for him to receive the state-sponsored HOPE College Scholarship. Our Ross was not only going to college, but he was going tuition-free! Not too bad considering, at times, we had our doubts that he would actually ever finish high school.

Jameson was a student at the University of Georgia, majoring in psychology. On his twenty-first birthday, he had an epiphany—he wanted to be a teacher. We teased that the thought of him shaping young minds was somewhat unsettling. In reality, we knew that he indeed had the personality for the job.

During the summer, Steve and I, along with Jameson and a college friend, headed west. Ross was invited, and encouraged, to join us. He chose instead to head up north with his friends, David and Aaron, to attend a music festival. The allure of seeing Ozzy Osbourne perform with the band Black Sabbath was apparently more overpowering than spending two weeks with his parents and his beloved brother.

Those of us who headed westward had an enjoyable vacation visiting Los Angeles, Las Vegas, and the Grand Canyon. While in L.A., Jameson was able to fulfill a lifelong dream—we had the pleasure of attending a taping of the game show The Price is Right.

Jameson had been an avid watcher of the show since he was a little boy, and he had always wanted to meet the host, Bob Barker. Unfortunately, members of the studio audience weren't allowed to meet Mr. Barker or take pictures of him. No matter. Just being able to watch the show's taping, and the interaction between Mr. Barker and the audience during commercial breaks, was good enough.

Although we had a great time on our trip, it wouldn't have been a true Atkinson event if everything had gone smoothly. Suffice it to say, we had enough to go wrong to fuel several events. In order not to bore you too much, here's a synopsis:

1. While in L.A., Jameson developed a line infection. His doctor in Georgia was able to order oral antibiotics at a local pharmacy in California.
2. Then, my aunt passed away, and I flew back to Georgia for her funeral. While there, I was able to pick up IV antibiotics for Jameson.
3. Due to a traffic accident that closed the interstate, I missed my flight back to Las Vegas and had to wait until the next morning to fly back.
4. Upon arriving in Vegas, I was able to spend one day with my husband before he had to fly back to Georgia for a vital work meeting.
5. Steve's flight back into Las Vegas was delayed, so it was well after nightfall when we began our drive to the Grand Canyon.
6. Around midnight, in the middle of the desolate desert, we discovered we were driving toward the wrong side of the canyon, which meant we were going in the wrong direction.
7. After backtracking for two hours, we finally discovered a motel and civilization, where we happily crashed for a few hours.
8. Finally made it to the Grand Canyon.

And that's how our family makes memories!

After summer travels were over, it was time for college. While Jameson's decision to change majors meant he had to begin taking education classes along with his psychology classes, Ross's decision to actually attend college had become a reality. Steve and I had been both shocked and pleased that he decided to further his education. We realized that Ross wasn't exactly studious, but we hoped he might find his niche in college. Also, not to sound too crass, but he would also be three hours away, and not living at home! After the battles we'd had, I felt we all needed a break from each other.

In October, we had received the official news that the plant at which Steve was manager was bought by a different company. In order for him to remain employed with Johnson & Johnson, we would have to move—again, to Pennsylvania. Although I really didn't want to make another move, I was more receptive to the idea than in the past. Both boys seemed to be doing well, physically and emotionally. Plus, Steve assured me that we would keep my farmhouse as our future retirement home.

Then came more news. Ross had arrived home for Christmas break. I was standing face to face with him, my hands planted firmly on his shoulders. Just minutes before, I had learned the final grades from his first semester in college—an F, a D, and a W (I later found out that he had also made one A). He had solemnly vowed that he would do much better the next semester. He attempted to explain that the first semester was a learning experience, a getting used to the whole college thing trial period.

Although I was extremely upset about his grades, standing there, looking at him, I believed he really would do better the next semester. I was trying to find the right words to say to him.

"Son," I began, "raising you is truly a..." and then the word just seemed to pop out, "privilege."

Privilege? Where on earth did that come from? That wasn't the word I was looking for!

Ross just stared at me and replied, "Okay."

Then we both walked our separate ways. As I went into the living room, I was still shaking my head. Privilege? I think the phrase I had been searching for was more along the lines of, "trying experience," "pain in the butt," "test of faith."

And then a thought struck me—raising him is a privilege. Raising both of my sons is truly a privilege that God has given me. Instead of looking at raising them as a chore, or exasperating, or difficult, I should always remember that God is allowing me to raise them. He has entrusted me to guide them into adulthood. That was indeed a very humbling thought.

CHAPTER 41

Yep. The year 2005 had been a wild ride, but the next couple of years proved to be even more trying. Steve moved back to Pennsylvania in January 2006. I decided to wait until the middle of March to join him. There were a few loose ends I needed to attend to at work. I also wanted to be around for a couple of months to make certain Ross stayed on the right track his second semester at school. He had finally made some good friends there, and seemed to be settling in, but I wanted to be available to him a bit longer.

Then on March 1, we received heartbreaking news: Steve's mom had died unexpectedly from a massive heart attack. I was at my parents' house for one last visit when Steve phoned me with the news. I was hesitant to convey the news to Ross and Jameson over the phone, but I felt they needed to know what had happened. I called Ross first. He was of course shocked, but he seemed more concerned with how Steve was doing. After unsuccessfully trying to reach Jameson a couple of times, I decided to wait and contact him the following morning, knowing that he had probably already gone to bed.

Around two thirty in the morning, my cell phone rang; it was Ross. He sounded panicky and wanted to know where I was. When I told him I was at my parents' house, and then asked him why he wanted to know, his reply overwhelmed me; and I began to cry. He explained that he knew I would be upset over Grandmama's death, so he had driven home from college to be with me. I had neglected to tell him that I was visiting with my parents for a few days. I felt horrible! I realized that he needed comforting, and there was no one to comfort him. I offered to drive home to be with him, but he assured me he would be all right. He said he felt exhausted and that he was going straight to bed. I can't begin to tell you how proud I was of my younger son that night.

Grandmama's sudden death affected all of us deeply, but especially Ross. He was not one to readily show outward emotion, but her death visibly took a toll on him throughout the days leading up to her funeral, as well as the funeral itself. Afterwards, in the following weeks, he appeared to pull himself together and move on with his predominately carefree life.

My move went without incident a couple of weeks later, and I quickly settled back into northern life. At the end of March, we received a call from Ross. He announced that he had done a lot of thinking, and he would not be returning to college his sophomore year. He had already virtually stopped attending his classes. He planned to stay at school for the remainder of the semester, but then he was done. Steve and I felt as though the sudden turn of events was directly related to lingering depression associated with Grandmama's death. We were disappointed with Ross's decision to drop out of college, but we were more concerned with his apparent lack of enthusiasm for the future.

I drove to Georgia the first week in May and helped Ross move out of the dorm. Although we tried to persuade him to move back in with us, he was very adamant about not living in Pennsylvania again. Since my beloved farmhouse was unoccupied, Ross deemed it as the perfect time to live on his own, while he tried to find himself.

"Living on his own" was actually a metaphorical phrase. In the beginning, he obviously had a high old time being on his own, while Steve and I provided all the necessities to sustain life. Over time, things began to change. He continued to have highs and lows, but soon the lows began to outweigh the highs.

In the meantime, Jameson seemed to be doing pretty well. He was enjoying his additional education classes, and his health appeared stable. Because of changing his major, he was now on the five year college plan instead of graduating in four. Also, he had made the decision to stick with psychology as his major. He had discovered several programs that would allow him to earn his teaching certification while working on his Master's degree in elementary education.

True, he had made two brief visits to the hospital due to IV line infections. Oh, and he was also hospitalized for a rare, life-threatening bacterial infection in his healthy large intestine. That little fiasco happened after an enjoyable day of swimming and jet skiing in one of the local lakes. The cause of the infection was never really determined, but the lake water was a prime suspect. Jameson had a history of presenting with symptoms and ailments that were abnormal to the common man.

Jameson also had impeccable timing. The above trip to the hospital coincided with a trip to Mexico City by Steve, Ross, and me. Steve had to travel there for business, so we decided to make it a mini family vacation. Jameson was unable to join us due to taking summer classes. Ross was beyond thrilled to go; he had always wanted to go to Mexico. We had enjoyed an entire twenty-four hours there when we received Jameson's phone call. He emphasized that we didn't need to alter our plans. My parents were with him, but they, along with the doctors, strongly suggested he call us. I immediately booked a flight to Georgia; Ross decided to accompany me back. By the time we arrived, the antibiotics were doing their job, and Jameson was feeling much better—another crisis under control.

Then, on a pleasant fall night in October, Jameson called to inform us that his portacath, which was implanted in his left inner bicep area, had mysteriously broken through the skin. He was freaked out! He took a picture of it and e-mailed it to us; then Steve and I were pretty freaked out. You could clearly see half of the IV port sticking out of his arm. After consulting with us, he headed to the ER. Ross met him there, to provide moral support.

After being evaluated, Jameson was told he had to go back home and return to the hospital the next morning in order for a radiologist to remove the port. Upon discussing the situation after his trip to the ER, the three of us were in agreement for him to forgo having another central line inserted after the port's removal. He wanted to see how well he could do without TPN for a while; Steve and I thought that was a good idea. The trick would be keeping his weight and lab values stable.

The boys traveled together to Pennsylvania in December to spend the holidays with us. They came for Christmas, probably because they wanted to make certain they received their gifts. They willingly stayed for New Year's Day in order to celebrate Steve's fiftieth birthday. We surprised him with a black 1979 Corvette as his birthday gift (he had always mourned the fact that I wouldn't let him buy one when we married). Ross and Jameson had pivotal roles in the gift presentation. Plus, they wanted a chance to ride in and drive it.

So, 2007 was off to a good start. The four of us had enjoyed the holidays together, and Jameson and Ross were able to ride nearly nineteen hundred miles in the same car without killing each other. I was also excited about my parents' fiftieth wedding anniversary reception that would take place in February. I had been working on the details with the caterer for several months, and I was looking very forward to everything coming together. Then there was the phone call.

After unsuccessfully taking care of himself, Ross came crashing down. It was difficult to piece together all of the details, but I knew for certain that Ross was hurting. For him to call me, and then breakdown on the phone while talking, meant that things were serious. Too much partying, and drinking, and self-destruction had taken their toll on our son. He was a mess, and my heart ached for him. I had learned that no matter how mad a parent could be, or how disappointed they were, it's still hard to see your child unhappy or hurting.

I flew to Georgia the next day; Ross picked me up at the airport. He seemed truly glad to see me. I didn't let anyone know that I was in town, or in the state, for that matter. I wanted to be able to devote the next few days entirely to Ross. After much discussion and encouragement from Steve and me, Ross decided it would be beneficial for him to move back to Pennsylvania for a while.

After my parents' reception (which was lovely, by the way), I returned home on a Tuesday, leaving Ross to pack-up and drive to our house on Saturday. I was somewhat reluctant to leave him for fear that he might change his mind and decide not to move. I decided to take his word and trust him. He arrived when he said he would. Two stipulations Steve and I had insisted on upon Ross's return to our home were one, he get a job, and two, he see a counselor on a regular basis. He had reluctantly agreed to both. The fun part would be making sure he followed through with each.

Within a week of Ross moving back in with us, we received a certified letter from the sheriff's office in our home county in Georgia. In summary, the letter stated that our property had been under surveillance for the distribution of illegal drugs. A search warrant had been served to Ross at our house on February 9. The entire property had been thoroughly searched by local DEA agents with drug sniffing canine. Since no illegal drugs or drug paraphernalia had been found, it had not been necessary to make any arrests, or seize our house and surrounding property. The case had been officially closed.

I sat there reading the letter in disbelief. I think I re-read it three or four times. The search had apparently taken place the day before Ross moved out. The icing on the cake was it had been Ross who signed for the letter on his way out, and then brought it back inside to me before he left. He had not mentioned the entire incident to either Steve or me after it occurred, or since he had moved back in with us.

After I had calmed myself down, I decided to call the commander of the drug task force who had written the letter. I needed to make certain that Ross was in the clear, but just as importantly that my property wasn't in danger of being seized. The officer was very blunt and not at all sympathetic to my plight. He even informed me that officers had been watching the house the entire time that I had been visiting there. I learned the case indeed was closed, but the entire scenario was still very unsettling to me.

When Ross returned home a short while later, I calmly asked him to have a seat. I then showed him the letter. After reading it he commented, "I wondered what that letter was about when I signed for it."

I exploded. "Why didn't you tell us about all of this?"

"I didn't see any need to. There was nothing for them to find," he replied.

We proceeded to talk for a long time. While I continued to be angry at him for neglecting to inform us concerning the entire incident, I couldn't help but be amazed at how he had kept his composure and had fully cooperated during the search. When I asked him if he had been scared, he replied that no, he wasn't, because he hadn't done anything wrong. He related how, after he answered their knock at the door and was served with the search warrant, one of the officers escorted him to the cottage and remained there with him throughout the property search. He went on to describe the entire search in detail. From Ross's account, the Drug Task Force did an extremely thorough job, inside and out. They were very upset to come up empty-handed. I was extremely thankful they did.

After a couple of months, the three of us were readjusting to living together again. Ross had a temporary job working full time, and he was meeting weekly with a therapist that he felt comfortable with. Ross and I even made use of two free airline tickets that I had by taking a trip to Los Angeles. We attended an open house at a film school, and then spent the next several days sightseeing. We visited numerous tourist attractions, including Hollywood, the Santa Monica Pier, and Disneyland. We had a surprisingly fun time, and we really enjoyed each other's company. It was refreshing to get away for a few days, and it was so nice to get along with each other. I hoped our family, as a whole, had hit a positive turning point.

Then, Jameson began having more health issues. He had been off of his TPN for about seven months, and had been doing well. In order to maintain a healthy weight while off of TPN, he was required to eat approximately 5,000 healthy calories per day, plus drink three liters of fluids. "Healthy" basically meant low fat and sugar, and high protein and carbohydrates. Jameson had given it a valiant try, but eventually, eating literally became a chore to him. He had grown tired of wondering what he was going to eat every two to three hours.

Gradually, his appetite diminished and he began losing weight; dehydration was also a major problem. Mental confusion, extreme drowsiness, and exhaustion were side effects of the dehydration. He was in his last semester of college, but some days he couldn't even make it out of bed to attend class. He began receiving extra IV fluids on an outpatient basis in an attempt to combat the dehydration, but he was losing the battle.

Although Steve and I had grown concerned over Jameson's health, we had no true idea to what extent it had nosedived. When he spent Easter with us in April, we could tell he had lost some weight over the past couple of months, but he still looked healthy. When we saw him one month later for his graduation, he looked entirely different. He had lost a large amount of weight, he looked very gaunt, and he appeared weak in general. It was as if once the weight began coming off, there was no stopping it.

The UGA graduation ceremony was nice, and we were extremely proud of Jameson's accomplishments, but the entire event was unusually taxing on him. The ceremony itself was held outside in the football stadium; the morning was very warm and humid. The graduates wore black caps and gowns, which only intensified the heat. Following the graduation, we had a luncheon at our farmhouse for friends and family in order to continue the celebration. Long time friends from Kentucky were visiting for the weekend, so we also had dinner reservations at a nice restaurant for that evening.

Jameson was so tired and out of sorts that he decided to take a short nap during the middle of his luncheon. He slept until nine o'clock that night. I realized then just how much his health had declined, and that something drastic had to be done.

Even in his deteriorated state of health, Jameson was very opposed to having yet another central IV line inserted and starting back on TPN. He simply couldn't admit to himself that his health was in such dire straits. After much discussion, I convinced him to at least have a feeding tube inserted into his abdomen so he could receive additional nutrition. The feeding could infuse throughout the night as he slept so as not to interfere with his daily life. Fortunately, Dr. Gunn was available to schedule and perform the procedure within a couple of days. I had begun a new job; therefore, I had to reluctantly return home to Pennsylvania the day after Jameson was discharged from the hospital.

Within two days of his release, he ended up back in the hospital due to his weakened condition. Steve and I were again extremely worried about him, so he drove back down to Georgia to be with Jameson. While there, Steve was able to convince him to travel back to Pennsylvania and spend a few weeks with us. In the meantime, I scheduled an appointment for Jameson with Dr. Lyn Howard, a renowned clinical nutritionist and GI specialist, associated with the Albany Medical Center in New York. I had met Dr. Howard at an Oley conference the previous summer.

If you recall, we first learned of the Oley Foundation back in 2002 when Jameson was a participant in the intestinal rehab program in Omaha. Finally, in 2006, Jameson and I had plans to attend the annual conference. An unplanned hospitalization thwarted his attendance, so I went on my own.

The Oley Foundation is a wonderful nonprofit organization that was established through private funding in 1983 by Dr. Howard and one of her patients, Clarence "Oley" Oldenburg. Its membership now surpasses eleven thousand. Oley provides information and psychosocial support to consumers who rely on home parenteral and/or enteral nutrition. In other words, Oley is a godsend to people, and their caregivers, who depend on IV and/or tube feedings as a means of life-sustaining nutrition. Attending that conference was truly a life-changing experience. I had the honor of meeting numerous individuals who lived each day with similar health and medical issues as Jameson. I realized immediately that we would no longer be traveling on our journey alone; those new friends would graciously be by our side.

The day before Jameson's appointment with Dr. Howard, a mere three days after arriving in PA, his weight had plummeted to 103 lbs. Since he had an early morning appointment, we decided to drive on up to Albany and spend the night. As evening melted away into night, so did Jameson's strength. He was barely able to hold his head up. We all went to bed early, hoping to get a good night's sleep. In the wee hours of the morning, Jameson futilely attempted to get out of bed and head to the bathroom. He was so weak and lethargic; Steve immediately decided we were taking him to the emergency room.

Steve and I were actually in fear for his life. We were in such a hurry, upon arrival at the ER, we didn't waste time retrieving a wheelchair. We literally lifted Jameson out of the car and carried him in. He was a mess. His blood pressure was low. His heart rate was extremely rapid. He was talking incoherently, and his speech was slurred. The nurse immediately started IV fluids and placed him on oxygen. After having blood work done, the lab results were horrible! If a value was normally low, his was sky-high. If the value should be elevated, Jameson's was rock bottom.

A while after the IV infusion was started, his vital signs had begun to stabilize. He was also speaking more clearly. Dr. Howard was notified that Jameson was being treated in the ER, so she came to see him there. She immediately began to work her magic. She basically told Jameson that since he was an adult, he needed to act like one. She reminded him that he was responsible for his own health, and he should be taking better care of himself. She talked with him, and us, for a long while. She even persuaded him to have a temporary central line inserted in order to get his nutritional status, and overall health, back on track. Jameson's appointment with Dr. Howard turned into a three day hospital stay, but it was well worth it.

Over the following weeks, Jameson's health did improve by leaps and bounds. He steadily gained weight and muscle mass; he no longer looked emaciated. His entire attitude and outlook improved. Also, during this ordeal, he learned he had been accepted into a Master's program in both Georgia and Pennsylvania. The three of us decided it would be in his best interest to move back in with us while he attended grad school. He hated the thought of leaving Athens, but he relished the idea of having a support system readily available. Jameson therefore accepted the offer from Holy Family University in Philadelphia and made his move back to PA at the end of August.

And then, once again, there were four.

CHAPTER 42

August 2007 – June 2012

Having the entire family living together again under the same roof was nice, but also proved to be somewhat of a challenge. Ross had quite enjoyed his stint as an "only child", so he was somewhat annoyed that Jameson had moved back in and was intruding on his turf. Likewise, Jameson at the age of twenty-three felt as though he was a fully vested adult, and really didn't need the advice of his parents. I'm not saying that he wasn't grateful for our support, but there were times that he didn't appreciate our opinions on any subject.

A memorable disagreement took place at the dinner table one pleasant summer evening. Steve was concerned that Jameson wasn't adhering to the level of medical compliance that he required. Jameson in turn became defensive and very argumentative about the subject. After several minutes of raised voices between the two, Jameson abruptly jumped up from the table and stormed out the front door. I recommended to Steve that we give him a chance to cool down and wait for him to come back inside.

Well, after several minutes had elapsed and he hadn't returned inside, Steve went out to try and smooth things over. A few minutes later Steve came back in and told me that Jameson was nowhere in sight. Although it was early September, the temperature was still pretty hot, and our intelligent, stubborn, health-compromised son had apparently decided to "go for a walk", without his cell phone or his shoes.

Steve and I looked at each other, went and got in the car, and proceeded to drive around. We drove through numerous neighborhoods, along well traveled and not-so well-traveled roads......no sign of Jameson. We then decided to make a sweep through the elementary school parking lot, and there he sat, on the curb, looking hot and exhausted. When asked if he wanted a ride home, (with his feet cut and sore) he didn't hesitate to climb into the car. He apologized for making us worry; he just needed to take a little walk to calm down and ended up walking a lot further than expected. It all ended well as Jameson did begin to step up his adherence to his health regime.

While Jameson adjusted to living with his family again, Ross continued to connect with old friends, make new acquaintances, and focus on his music. He worked for a while, then felt as though he needed something else. With the encouragement of a friend, he decided to give college another try. He enrolled at the local community college, and although some of his classes were perceived as boring and mundane, his grades were really good.

Jameson graduated from Holy Family University in May of 2009 with a Master's Degree in Elementary Education. Steve and I, along with my parents, were beaming with pride when he received his Diploma! He celebrated his accomplishment by going sky diving with his dad, something both of them had always talked about doing. Steve and I really tried to convince him to stay in Pennsylvania to teach, considering all of the good contacts he had made during his two years of substitute teaching, but his mind was set. Jameson promptly packed up and moved back to Georgia.

Ross, after completing a year of community college and discovering that being back in school wasn't so bad, transferred with his girlfriend to West Virginia University. They rented an apartment together and were ready to conquer the world. But the world in West Virginia proved to be different from the world in Pennsylvania. Let's just say that going to a large college in a small party town is entirely different from a very small community college close to home.

After a year and a half in West Virginia, Ross was ready to return home. He and his girlfriend had parted ways, the stress of living on his own had become overwhelming, and the constant partying to numb his loneliness was becoming detrimental. Upon returning home he took a few weeks to settle back in and reconnect with old friends, and then he found a full-time job.

In June of 2011, Ross followed his brother and also re-established his roots in Georgia. After a few months, not only were Jameson and Ross both back in Georgia, but were again living in the Athens area. An important fact to mention is that the two of them no longer had a strong dislike for each other. Oh sure, they'd still roll their eyes at each other's comments, or each would make sure the other knew how stupid an idea sounded, but that's what siblings do. They still don't always see eye to eye, but now they are brothers who have become friends.

As their mother, I was really hopeful that with Jameson and Ross living close together that they would become even better friends. Of course, God seemed to have other plans in mind....

Jameson had worked steadily as a substitute teacher after moving back to Athens, but hadn't been able to land a full-time teaching position in the midst of state wide budget crunches. He really enjoyed working with elementary-age students so he wasn't willing to apply for middle or high school positions. The situation placed him in a dilemma due to his medical issues. He really wanted to be totally independent, which included him being able to maintain his own health insurance.

Then he did the unbelievable by applying for a full-time position with a major insurance company located in another part of the state! When the job was offered to him, he readily accepted. No one could believe that he was going to move from his beloved Athens, but he was determined.

Jameson would be working for a well-established company with a good reputation and one that also offered opportunity for career advancement and a good benefits package. But the really amusing part was the actual location of his job.......he would be moving to my hometown of Macon. And not only was it my birthplace, but Steve had also been born there. Jameson would be living in the city where I grew up. The place where my parents, his grandparents, still lived. The area where most of mine and Steve's relatives still lived. The place where I had met Steve, where we dated, fell in love, and got married and began our life together. Jameson was moving to the place where the story of our little family actually began.

Norman Rockwell would probably have reminded me that art really does imitate life....

EPILOGUE

Some pages of this book were written with tears streaming down my face, some with a huge smile of remembrance, and some with an absolute feeling of wonderment. All of them were written with a mother's unwavering love and devotion. I am so thankful for my children, but I'm equally grateful that they were brought back to me from the brinks of death and self-destruction.

Although both sons are now adults, I realize that my responsibility to help guide them will never end. Because I'm their parent, I will always give them advice, solicited or unsolicited, and will try to direct them in the path that I feel is most beneficial. My views are not always met with open arms or open minds, and that's okay. For example, I'd often encouraged Jameson to work toward decreasing the quantity of TPN that he takes, mainly due to the possible long-term ill effects that TPN can have on liver function. He, on the other hand, was very content with his TPN regimen, and it was his decision to make.

Then a new injectable medication, Gattex, was approved by the FDA for the purpose of increasing the absorption capacity of the small intestine in people living with Short Bowel Syndrome, therefore reducing the need for TPN. This was indeed very exciting news! After waiting several months to see how other TPN users were responding to the medication, Jameson made the decision to apply for permission to receive the drug.

It was wonderful news when he was granted approval! He continues to infuse a bag of IV fluids several nights per week to maintain hydration and vitamin & mineral requirements. The important thing is he no longer requires the lipids, which are the main culprits of liver damage.

I also wish that Ross had earned his college degree; I would have been happy with any degree! After attending three different colleges in three different states, and numerous unsuccessful attempts made to convince him to go back, just one more time, getting that degree apparently wasn't meant to be. Ross is satisfied with his choice, and it is his choice. So, I've come to accept the fact that it's alright to disagree.

Somewhere along the way, life in the Atkinson family has actually mellowed, somewhat. That doesn't mean the past several years have been problem-free. Oh, I know every family has its share of problems, and I definitely know mine pale in comparison to the vast majority. Still, every time my phone rings late at night, or I hear the "ding" of an incoming text message in the middle of the night, I immediately expect the worse, and my stomach knots up in anticipation of what news awaits on the other end.

Ross and Jameson have both had their share of mountains and valleys over the years. They've had broken dreams, broken relationships, and broken spirits, but they do manage to "rise from the ashes" and move on. They also will each occasionally veer off in a totally diverse direction—take the road less traveled. Then, they each find themselves somewhere new, and a different chapter in their life begins.

Thankfully, both sons have experienced a very pivotal event in each of their lives. On June 17, 2014, Dorothy Grace Starstuff Davis Atkinson entered this world (I know, that's a big name for a little girl, but she has enough personality to handle it!), and Ross became a dad! Dory loves her Daddy, and her Daddy loves her! She is a beautiful, sweet, inquisitive, energetic, smart, precious child, and she reminds us so much of her daddy when he was a little boy. Dory makes our world such a better, happier place to live.

Then, on November 4, 2017, Jameson married his love, Ivy, and our family gained a beautiful new member. The two of them are, as the saying goes, "made for each other". Ivy takes all of Jameson's quirks and medical issues in stride, and now she's the one who helps him keep his health in check instead of Steve and I. The two of them together prove how enjoyable traveling through this crazy life can be.

A friend once questioned why Ross was allowed to get away with inappropriate behavior, time and time again. The point was made that Steve and I had to have known that he was manipulating us, yet we never seemed to make him face the consequences for his actions. Wouldn't our life have been much easier if we had followed through with more of our threats?

I honestly didn't have the answer to her questions, and I still don't. Steve and I were very unsure of how to handle a lot of the situations we found ourselves in with Ross. His rebellion and disrespect tore at our very souls, but we were determined not to give up on him. You always think you know how you would respond to and deal with specific situations. Then when they actually do happen, you find yourself unsure of your convictions, and you're virtually helpless. To paraphrase an old saying—you really can't condemn another person until you take a walk in their shoes.

In hindsight, I'm sure I should have been more strict, but I was a coward. I hated the confrontations, the destruction of property. I despised Ross's outbursts, but it was even more unsettling when he kept his emotions inward. Although several therapists deemed him of no harm to himself or others, I always feared there would be that one time when Ross would abandon all logic, and he would attempt to take his precious life. I could not be the one to set that scenario in motion. My love for both of my sons is unconditional, no matter what the situation. I don't always like them, but I never don't love them. Steve has always commented that one son is his heart, and one is his soul, and that both his heart and soul have been torn apart before. That's how it feels to love your children.

I also believe that God has extended his grace to us, as a family, and has showered us with his love time and time again. Although I know we are continually undeserving of his favor, he keeps blessing us anyway. The blessings are sometimes overlooked, but they are there. And God's blessings in our lives take many shapes and forms, from the miraculous saving of a son's life after a medical catastrophe, to "hiding" car keys in plain sight from a son too drunk to drive. I believe God shows us, as parents, His grace and mercy in order that we'll know how to reflect it onto our children. And although we go through trials that we can't understand, and our faith wavers, we have to learn that God remains faithful to us.

I try not to dwell on Jameson's health. Some days, there seem to be constant reminders; other days, I barely [even] think about it. We even celebrate May 2 as Jameson's rebirth day, instead of dreading it as a reminder each year. But it always seems to be there, in the back of my mind. For years, I couldn't comprehend how something so tragic could have happened to my child. He hadn't done anything to deserve that type of tragedy to befall him! Then one day, the answer became clearly apparent to me; it was as if God Himself had tapped me on the shoulder…No one's child deserves pain, or illness, or suffering. My child is no more precious than anyone else's. Strangely, that revelation somehow gave me a sense of contentment and a truer understanding of God's love.

I have a dear friend whose own son tragically suffered an anoxic brain injury while playing a simple game of soccer with a group of friends. Jonathan was starting his final year of college as an engineering major. He was a brilliant mathematician and simply a joy to be around. He is now unable to communicate or move on his own, thus requiring total care. Something he can do is smile and laugh at things that amuse him. Lois is a very devoted Christian and mother. She has lamented that she doesn't understand why God allows certain things to happen, but she does know she just has to keep trusting Him anyway. And through that trust, comes peace.

Maybe that's the simple answer to all of our hard questions.[1]

ENDNOTES

1 "It is Well with My Soul"

   Words: Horatio Spafford, 1873

   Music: Philip Bliss, 1876

   Job: Biblical character in the Old Testament who had his righteousness tested by disaster and personal affliction.

   Anoxic brain injury: Loss of brain cells due to lack of oxygen

   For more information about The Oley Foundation, please visit their website at www.oley.org

www.ingramcontent.com/pod-product-compliance
Lightning Source LLC
Chambersburg PA
CBHW021441070526
44577CB00002B/242